Civic Apps Competition Handbook

Kate Eyler-Werve and Virginia Carlson

O'REILLY®

Beijing · Cambridge · Farnham · Köln · Sebastopol · Tokyo

Civic Apps Competition Handbook

by Kate Eyler-Werve and Virginia Carlson

Published by O'Reilly Media, Inc., 1005 Gravenstein Highway North, Sebastopol, CA 95472.

O'Reilly books may be purchased for educational, business, or sales promotional use. Online editions are also available for most titles (*http://my.safaribooksonline.com*). For more information, contact our corporate/institutional sales department: 800-998-9938 or *corporate@oreilly.com*.

Editors: Julie Steele and Meghan Blanchette	**Proofreader:** O'Reilly Production Services
Production Editor: Kristen Borg	**Cover Designer:** Karen Montgomery
	Interior Designer: David Futato
	Illustrator: Rebecca Demarest

Revision History for the First Edition:

2012-09-07   First release

See *http://oreilly.com/catalog/errata.csp?isbn=9781449322649* for release details.

ISBN: 978-1-449-32264-9

[LSI]

Table of Contents

Preface

"Data, data, data! I cannot make bricks without clay!"
—SHERLOCK HOLMES

A Practical Guide for Organizing a Civic Apps Competition

Government agencies are increasingly being called upon to publish data as a means to increase transparency, deliver government services more efficiently, and innovate business. Civic Apps Competitions (CACs) further these goals by providing incentives and a platform for software programmers to build innovative applications ("apps") using open government data. Departments at all levels are proactively using technology to share their data with the public, through the "low tech" release of spreadsheet or database files to the "high tech" release of data through Application Programming Interfaces (API) and associated "apps competitions."

While the technological problems of these competitions are (largely) solved—a plethora of content management systems and turn-key web software-as-service platforms can easily handle the requirements of submitting projects, collecting public votes, etc.—what has become important is ensuring that the outcomes of these competitions return value. Governments, civic activists, and software developers who have invested or are thinking of investing in open government data want answers to long-term questions. How, and under what conditions, do open data result in high-quality platforms relevant to problems at hand? Are the resulting applications sustainable in a way that will continue to deliver solutions over time? Do the competitions themselves foster transparency and engagement for a wide audience?

When Chicago's Mayor Rahm Emanuel took office on May 16, 2010, he put launching a civic apps competition on his first 100 days checklist. Five weeks later, the Apps for Metro Chicago (A4MC) competition launched. When we started planning A4MC in late May, there were no formal agreements between any of the partners; by June, Mayor Emanuel was on the cover of the local daily paper, challenging civic coders to compete for $50,000 in prizes. We learned a lot. We'd like to share it.

This book is a practical guide to planning a civic apps competition (CAC). We aren't just relying on our own experience with A4MC though; we surveyed 15 CACs hosted in the United States and Canada over the last three years. As a result, we've uncovered some surprising insights into what makes competitions successful. And, of course, we've got anecdotes of budget overruns and political infighting (and some fun success stories) to keep it interesting.

This Guide identifies a number of ways to ensure an apps competition delivers on the goals of accountability, government efficiency and economic innovation.

A note on the open government movement and the use of terms. *Open government* is a movement that demands transparency from governments regarding actions and decisions, increasing the government's accountability. *Open government data* refers to the specific practice of publishing data collected by governments in order to facilitate transparency, create efficiencies and prime economic innovation. CACs are designed to kickstart the use of open government data. Throughout this guide, we'll use the shorter-termed "open data" or "open civic data" when talking about open government data.

This Guide

This guide is broadly sectioned into four parts. We start off in Chapter 1 by giving a bit of history of Civic Apps Competitions and what critiques have been leveled at the competitions and their outcomes. In Chapter 2 we then challenge the cynics with what we see as benefits of CACs. If executed correctly and with the right expectations, competitions can set the stage for more civic interaction, better delivery of government services, and become a staging ground for improving private- and non-profit-business.

If you're up and ready to start a competition, however, feel free to jump to Chapter 3. Here you'll find a juicy discussion of translating benefits into goals and metrics. In a data-driven world, shouldn't we have data by which to track the success of CACs? And, you'll likely need hard numbers to report out to funders or government agencies. We give some ideas as to how to measure processes and outcomes. Chapter 4 discusses what it actually takes to run a competition, putting dollar figures to specific activities. A4MC, with prizes, cost over a quarter-million dollars. But there are ways to cut that number.

We then turn to nuts and bolts. What data works for CACs? Chapter 5 discusses different kinds of open government data and what's likely to jumpstart your competition. Chapter 6 reveals the finer points of CACs—process, judging, rules, and the legal fine print.

Chapter 7 and Chapter 8 are summary chapters. We set aside Chapter 7 as a place to summarize some of the common roadblocks we and others encountered. Feel free to jump to this chapter if you're in the middle of designing your own competition and want a quick checklist on what you might have missed. Chapter 8 speculates on the future for your competition and CACs in general.

Contact Us

We continue to be deeply interested in the potential for open government data to be harnessed for the common good. Virginia Carlson has worked in the government data world since starting Chicago's first-ever public-serving DataBank at the University of Illinois-Chicago two decades ago. Look for her on the Board of Directors for the Association of Public Data Users, or on Twitter (@VL_Carlson). Kate Eyler-Werve gleefully seeks out disruptive technologies to work on and can project manage anything. You can find her at www.eylerwerve.com.

Conventions Used in This Book

The following typographical conventions are used in this book:

Italic
> Indicates new terms, URLs, email addresses, filenames, and file extensions.

Using Code Examples

This book is here to help you get your job done. In general, you may use the code in this book in your programs and documentation. You do not need to contact us for permission unless you're reproducing a significant portion of the code. For example, writing a program that uses several chunks of code from this book does not require permission. Selling or distributing a CD-ROM of examples from O'Reilly books does require permission. Answering a question by citing this book and quoting example code does not require permission. Incorporating a significant amount of example code from this book into your product's documentation does require permission.

We appreciate, but do not require, attribution. An attribution usually includes the title, author, publisher, and ISBN. For example: "*Civic Apps Competition Handbook* by Kate Eyler-Werve and Virginia Carlson (O'Reilly). Copyright 2012 Virginia Carlson, Katherine Eyler-Werve, 978-1-449-32264-9."

If you feel your use of code examples falls outside fair use or the permission given above, feel free to contact us at *permissions@oreilly.com*.

Safari® Books Online

 Safari Books Online (*www.safaribooksonline.com*) is an on-demand digital library that delivers expert content in both book and video form from the world's leading authors in technology and business.

Technology professionals, software developers, web designers, and business and creative professionals use Safari Books Online as their primary resource for research, problem solving, learning, and certification training.

Safari Books Online offers a range of product mixes and pricing programs for organizations, government agencies, and individuals. Subscribers have access to thousands of books, training videos, and prepublication manuscripts in one fully searchable database from publishers like O'Reilly Media, Prentice Hall Professional, Addison-Wesley Professional, Microsoft Press, Sams, Que, Peachpit Press, Focal Press, Cisco Press, John Wiley & Sons, Syngress, Morgan Kaufmann, IBM Redbooks, Packt, Adobe Press, FT Press, Apress, Manning, New Riders, McGraw-Hill, Jones & Bartlett, Course Technology, and dozens more. For more information about Safari Books Online, please visit us online.

How to Contact Us

Please address comments and questions concerning this book to the publisher:

O'Reilly Media, Inc.
1005 Gravenstein Highway North
Sebastopol, CA 95472
800-998-9938 (in the United States or
Canada)
707-829-0515 (international or local)
707-829-0104 (fax)

We have a web page for this book, where we list errata, examples, and any additional information. You can access this page at *http://oreil.ly/civic-apps-comp-hb*.

To comment or ask technical questions about this book, send email to *bookques tions@oreilly.com*.

For more information about our books, courses, conferences, and news, see our website at *http://www.oreilly.com*.

Find us on Facebook: *http://facebook.com/oreilly*

Follow us on Twitter: *http://twitter.com/oreillymedia*

Watch us on YouTube: *http://www.youtube.com/oreillymedia*

CHAPTER 1

The Pursuit of Accountability, Efficiency, and Economic Growth

History of Apps Contests

Apps for Metro Chicago (A4MC) was two years in the making. Several groups, including the Chicago Tribune Apps Development team, the Open Government Data Meet-up, and the Metro Chicago Information Center (MCIC), had been pushing the city to publish data and host an associated apps competition for two years with no luck.

Executive Director of MCIC, Virginia Carlson, had agreed to have MCIC take on the task of running the competition, especially given that many wanted Chicago's app contest to specifically reach out to community organizations and be able to offer technical assistance to teams. MCIC had even received funding to run the competition from the John D. and Catherine T. MacArthur Foundation, but the MCIC was holding on to it until Mayor Richard Daley pulled the trigger or a new mayor was elected.

So everyone was thrilled sideways when Mayor Rahm Emanuel made open government data and an associated Civic Apps Competition (CAC) a priority. Kate Eyler-Werve became the competition project manager a month before the launch and we were off. A4MC was launched in June of 2011.

The first government competition, "Apps for Democracy," was sponsored by Washington D.C. in 2008. The contest was initiated by Vivek Kundra, then chief technology officer for the District of Columbia (he later became the first-ever Federal Chief Information Officer), and designed and executed by digital marketing agency iStrategyLabs. Participants had one month to build apps that addressed a range of citizen needs, like bike routes, crime hot spots, and neighborhood amenities. Apps for Democracy attracted 47 entries, thus demonstrating that software developers would donate their time and energy to build engaging web and mobile applications that used municipal data feeds.

The success of Apps for Democracy inspired a host of state and municipal governments to launch their own competitions, including San Francisco, Portland, New York City, and Chicago of course, as well as the states of California and Illinois. Several Federal government departments, including the USDA and the EPA, have launched their own challenges, and the Federal government created an online challenge platform, Challenge.gov, in 2010 to support smaller challenges.

CACs and Goals—Do They Deliver?

Now, four years into a flurry of apps competitions and a lot of public interest, some question whether or not CACs actually deliver increased transparency, government efficiency, and innovation. Let's unpack these critiques.

Transparency and accountability

Open data is often criticized for not delivering on government accountability goals. But making data available is only one part of the accountability process. Open data needs to be tied to an accountability "mechanism" in order to achieve accountability. For example, if a government provides a data stream about planned infrastructure improvements, but there's no way for citizens to weigh in on priorities, you perhaps have transparency but not accountability.

From our perspective, the accountability mechanism doesn't have to be "new." One of the themes upon which conducted our Apps Competition and that we'll stress in this guide is that there's an existing multitude set of orgs that have traditionally used government data to scrutinize government. These orgs should intentionally be made part of open government contests and campaigns: journalists, community organizers, better-government associations, civic watchdog groups, etc.

Having software developers and data analysts working directly with such civic stakeholder groups increases the possibility that what's revealed by the data will get used for accountability. What A4MC did to address this was to give additional judging points to apps that came from partnerships that included a civic stakeholder groups. We also set up what we termed "Hack Salons" which brought together community orgs with software developers around specific issues. We learned that there is mutual suspicion –civic coders expected the community organizations wanted "something for free" and community organizations were loath to give time to something that they thought was a "gimmick." It took effort to learn to speak both languages and find common ground. The idea lives on in Code for America-sponsored Chicago Civic Idea Hack (ideahackchicago.com).

Yet even where an accountability mechanism exists, the data sometimes could be more complete in terms of contributing to transparency. Such was the case in Chicago when Mayor Daley opened one of the first data sets, a list of all Freedom of Information Act (FOIA) requests submitted to the city. However, the data did not include a field noting whether or not the request had been fulfilled. So everyone could see what people were requesting, but there was no way to determine if the city was actually fulfilling those requests. Incomplete data. The City of Chicago addressed that problem to some extent by hiring a Chief Data Officer (Brett Goldstein) whose job it was to proactively participate in "citizen data" sessions and otherwise listen for what was missing in data. Goldstein took it upon himself to attend hackathons, Hack Salons, tech conferences, Meetup groups and the like to hear what folks were saying about the City's data.

The potential for accountability also depends on the kind of data that is made available. We'll discuss different kinds of data in Ch. 6, but in short, sometimes data just doesn't lend itself to citizen engagement. Consider geographic data like elevations or census tract boundaries—this information might be necessary to build apps, but in itself doesn't engage citizens on any particular issue.

Government efficiency

A common critique of CACs is that apps created by competitions face hurdles to long-run sustainability and thus struggle to affect government efficiency. It's tough to know the extent of the drop-off, however because contest coordinators have not required app developers to run or submit analytics. As Peter Corbett has suggested "One lesson I've learned is we don't really know [how many are still functional two years later] because we don't have the analytics for each of the apps. If you're running an application development challenge, it would be great to give your developers individual Google Analytics codes so you can track usage. We didn't do that."[1]

A major challenge is that government procurement rules prevent apps created by CACs to be quickly adopted by government agencies. For example, "truck route finder," a cool app developed for A4MC, was meant to be adopted by the city's industrial corridors as a way to help trucks avoid low viaducts and street closures, find gasoline stations, and generally assist truck drivers as they navigate the city. Such an app would be a tremendous help to the city in terms of competing for industrial jobs. Yet the software, although developed with input from the industrial corridor managers, had not been acquired through the official procurement process and therefore could not be brought in-house.

In addition, there is pressure on CTOs and CIOs to concentrate their efforts on opening up government data and leaving the development of the apps themselves to (non-governmental) local developers. There's tension between the goals of government

---

1. *http://radar.oreilly.com/2010/05/government-innovation-from-the.html*

efficiency and spurring innovation. If government builds the app and it addresses an efficiency goal, it might be at the (perceived or real) expense of supporting innovation among local software developers. A heated argument ensured in the winter of 2011-12 when the City of Chicago for Chicago released an app for snowplow tracking.[2] A debate about the role of government and government workers among local open civic data enthusiasts ensued. Some argued that the City was right to take the lead on some app generation; others argued for a more government-hands-off approach.

Logan Kleier, Portland's CISO, supports the notion that one way to make open government data competitions more sustainable is by engaging the government workforce. "Starting with a small group of departments who might not know that their data could be useful to each other would be a good first step," Kleier said in an interview.[3] In addition, state law usually prevents government workers from entering a competition itself because the government is a partner in the CAC. We had to disqualify a fabulous app for manufacturing site locators because it was developed by an agency associated with the City.

The right balance has to be found between "gov development" and "civic coder development" to get usable apps with potential for government adaption.

More recently there's been some discussion about the problem of bringing apps to a scale which would create broader governmental efficiencies. As Mike Mathieu suggests, "[s]imply put, civic apps don't roam across political jurisdictions."[4] Just think, for example, how much more useful the A4MC "truck route finder" could be if the developer was able to integrate data from across regional governments—viaduct clearances not just in Chicago, but also in cities between the highway and Chicago industrial areas.

Private sector activity

Still others have pointed out that few private sector businesses have been built as a result of an apps competition. Although open government data has been conceived as a platform upon which to build "a rising tide of entrepreneurship,"[5] so far the number of businesses arising out of a CAC is small. NYC BigApps 1.0 winner MyCityWay won millions in venture capital and now covers 70 cities. A4MC winner SpotHero won a place in Excelerate, a tech incubator that provides mentorship and funding to promising start-ups. Nevertheless, there is no guarantee CACs themselves will launch new businesses.

2. *http://gridchicago.com/2012/plow-tracker-not-ready-for-prime-time/*

3. Personal communication, July 15, 2012

4. *http://techpresident.com/news/22298/three-problems-civic-hackathons*

5. *http://www.whitehouse.gov/innovationfellows/opendata*

One private sector success related to Civic Apps Competitions is the increased usage and popularity of Socrata, Inc., based in Seattle Washington which provides the technology backbone for governments to release open data. It powers a plethora of local initiatives including Chicago, Portland, San Francisco and New York (it also powers many of the federal government's open data websites including data.gov).

Competition ROI

Apps for Democracy famously cost Washington D.C.'s Office of the Chief Technology Officer $50,000. D.C.'s CTO estimated that the value of the apps created was $2.3 million, a 4000% return on investment.[6]

These numbers have doubtless been cited in support of hosting apps competitions launched since then—we certainly included them in our Apps for Metro Chicago proposal. However, a closer analysis of the ROI claim reveals flaws in calculating both the value of the apps created and the cost of hosting a competition

The CTO calculated the value of apps by estimating the market value of the hours worked, then adding the external contracting costs and internal time that procuring the apps would have required. But there is no reason to think that DC would have procured every single one of the apps submitted to the competition. Furthermore, this calculation assumed that all the apps would be sustained over time. Thus, the value of the submitted apps to Washington DC was over-stated.

And then there is the question of the "investment" —the cost of hosting the month-long competition. Apps for Democracy was hosted by Washington D.C.'s office of the Chief Technology Officer, but it was actually run by digital marketing firm iStrategyLabs. A close read of the reports on the outcomes of the competition shows that the only costs counted are those borne by the Office of the Chief Technology Officer. As MCIC found, there is a great potential for hidden "in kind" costs in a competition (hosting civic hackathons, media engagement, venues for awards ceremonies, etc.) so that the "real" budget could have been over $50,000.

What is at issue here is the trade-off between a quick ROI and a long-run payoff. Real development of apps that are effective and sustainable and build a community of users is, as we discuss in the following chapters, difficult and expensive. When Bryan Sivak took the CTO office in 2009 he declined to run Apps for Democracy for what would have been its third year. At the time he was reported to not have "[given] up on the idea of engaging smart and creative software developers for the public good; he simply wants a more meaningful relationship with them."[7] What MCIC learned from trying to do just

6. Corbett, 2009 (*http://www.appsfordemocracy.org/*)

7. *http://www.governing.com/topics/technology/Government-Apps-Move-from.html*

that—develop a meaningful relationship with software developers—is that that approach ran us $300,000 (we discuss our costs in Chapter 4). Outreach to community groups, sustaining public interest through three rounds meant to build time for continued app improvement, partner coordination and all the rest is time-consuming.

Next Chapter: What CACs Create

As we've seen, the traditional goals of CACs—supporting transparency, efficiency and economic growth—are problematic. But problematic isn't the same as wrong. In the next chapter we'll show how CACs do help governments meet those goals.

CHAPTER 2

Benefits of Civic Apps Competitions

Apps for Democracy was followed by the Sunlight Labs competition "Apps for America" in 2009. Clay Johnson, in charge of the competition, continues to work in the open government space. He says, and our experience with A4MC compels us to agree, that the point of open data "isn't to litter the web full of disposable web apps that are soon forgotten about. It's to build sustained developer interest around this data." John Tolva, Chicago's Chief Technology Officer is of the same mind. After A4MC ended he said, "The apps were fantastic, but the real output of A4MC was the community of urbanists and coders that came together to create them."

We can talk about this process as building a "community of practice," an informal network of peers with different skills, learning about a common subject together. It's not enough just to know about the data; in a community of practice, people use it.

Civic Apps Competitions (CACs) can do this - focus attention and interest on civic data and create an arena where people's creativity and work are recognized and shared. A well designed CAC engages non-profits, businesses, government departments and community organizations, as well as developers. It may in the process create "app litter," but can also focus on building connections for long-run development.

The problem is, the benefits of engaging a community of practice around open data aren't as easy to quantify as a simple return on investment metric. We found, and believe others have too, that there are other less-quantifiable goals.

We've broken out the three broad goals outlined in Chapter 1 into seven outcomes that can be evaluated:

Accountability
1. Raise awareness of available open government data sources
2. Focus energy on building apps on open data
3. Improve government transparency by making open data accessible

Government Efficiency
4. Create apps that benefit people and businesses
5. Crowdsource data publishing priorities

Economic Development
6. Drive innovation
7. Build a community of practice around open government data

We'll explore these seven outcomes in detail later in this chapter, but we'd like to start with a story. Elizabeth Park's experience with Apps for Metro Chicago illustrates how participating in a CAC brings new people into a community of practice around open government data.

Case Study

In the summer of 2011, Elizabeth Park was the Marketing Director for the American Society for Clinical Pathology in Chicago. Six months later she had launched two mobile apps: IFindit Chicago and IFindit Illinois. What happened in between? She entered the Apps for Metro Chicago Competition.

Elizabeth first learned about the Apps for Metro Chicago Competition (A4MC) at TechWeek Chicago, a technology and entrepreneurship conference. She went because she likes to learn what's current, and to brush up her professional skills. Most of the presentations were too technical for her, but then she made a connection with someone on the A4MC panel.

The competition had just launched and the audience was full of developers peppering Chicago's Chief Data Officer Brett Goldstein with questions about the types of apps the city wanted. Goldstein turned the questions right back on the audience, pointing out that the city wanted to mine the creativity and participation of its citizens. What do the people want? Elizabeth was blown away: "He was throwing down the gauntlet and challenging people to get involved with open data," she said.

Elizabeth decided to enter the competition then and there. "I thought, 'what can I lose?' I can do something civic, something I care about. It just made me want to do something really interesting," she said. She liked that the challenge was structured as a competition, because it provided a timeline with a definitive end point. It's easier to try something new when there's a goal and an incentive, in this case a shot at winning the Community category.

Elizabeth went to the database and was immediately struck by the amount of data about food, clinics and shelter. She called the Women, Infants and Children Program of Chicago (WIC) to see if the program was using any those data sets. WIC is a federal grant program that provides food, education and health care referrals to low-income new mothers and young children. As she investigated, Elizabeth discovered that WIC did not use the data, but that program participants frequently ask about clinics, shelter and food—information that could be provided through the data.

Next, she checked the A4MC website, which included a list of apps suggestions submitted by the public. Matt Peron, treasurer at Illinois Hunger, had submitted an idea for an app that mashed up city data on public services.

Elizabeth had hit on a problem in need of a solution. WIC and Illinois Hunger could better serve their constituents if they could easily and quickly provide information about a range of public services. So she decided to build an app that could just that.

Her next step was to decide whether to build a mobile or a web app. Her goal was to make a tool that people could use directly, so she did some research and found that 70% of low income people have a cell phone, and 50% of people making under $30,000 a year have a smart phone. So she challenged herself to make a mobile app—a challenge all the more impressive because she didn't know how to write a single line of code.

Now she needed to build a team. She knew she couldn't afford to hire an experienced professional, so she went to the Illinois Institute of Technology resume book of recent graduates. She made some calls and found Laura Guenther, a user interface specialist who was developing iPad apps for Kraft Foods that help kids learn about making healthy choices. Laura was interested in building useful civic apps, so she teamed up with Elizabeth and brought in another developer to write the code.

It took the group seven or eight weeks to build iFinditChicago.com, a mobile app to "serve Chicagoans by providing quick information regarding access to food, shelter and medical care in their area." All three team members were working full time jobs throughout the project. Elizabeth's experience was "a big leap of faith for me," she said. "I had no experience managing a tech team."

Elizabeth asked Matt Peron from Illinois Hunger to serve as a beta tester. He not only agreed, he rounded up several other organizations to help test, too. Ultimately WIC, the Illinois Hunger Coalition, the Heartland Alliance, Feeding America and the Greater Chicago Food Depository all agreed to beta test the app.

The team's hard work paid off; they won first prize in A4MC's community app challenge. But that was just the start for Elizabeth and her team. Elizabeth was invited to present iFinditChicago.com to the Illinois Innovation Council, a group of leaders convened by Governor Pat Quinn to advance the innovation economy. Brad Keywell, the co-founder of Groupon was impressed with her research. Until then he didn't know the stats on low income smart phone adoption. That experience really resonated with Elizabeth: "Until we realize how people use tools, we're going to miss opportunities," she said.

As a result of her presentation, Governor Quinn introduced Elizabeth to Illinois Chief Information Officer Sean Vink, to expand the app to cover all of Illinois. She was also connected to the state Commission to End Hunger. As a result, Elizabeth launched iFinditIllinois.com on February 8th, 2012—just 6 months after she first heard about Apps for Metro Chicago.

Since A4MC, Elizabeth has been contacted St. Anthony, a homeless outplacement hospital in San Francisco, to build a similar app for the Northern California city. She has also been talking with Streetwise, a magazine dedicated to helping the homeless in Chicago, to discuss how it might use technology to better serve its mission.

Today Elizabeth is a regular presence at local hackathons and tech meet-ups. "Entering A4MC irreversibly put me on a new course—it laid the foundation for Act 2 of my career, which is socially/civic minded solutions using technology to scale impact," she said. "It inspired me to think outside of my 9 to 5 job. I have a lot to contribute. I can create a viable product. It's hard to believe that back in June I'd never even dabbled in this!"

What Civic Apps Competitions Achieve

We like this case study because it beautifully illustrates the range of benefits that apps competitions can create. Let's take them one by one.

Accountability

1. Raise awareness of available open government data sources

Clearly Elizabeth and her team became aware of open government data through the competition. But one of the most interesting points in this case study is the list of institutions that were either unaware of available and potentially helpful open government data, or simply weren't using it. WIC, Illinois Hunger, the Heartland Alliance, Feeding America and the Greater Chicago Food Depository all discovered open data resources as a result of A4MC.

2. Focus energy on building apps on open data

The difference between an awareness campaign and an apps competition is that the competition provides a structure that supports building projects. Elizabeth liked the timeline because it motivated and organized her team. The competition also provided several incentives: winning apps would get both recognition and prize money. While Elizabeth's team was primarily motivated by a desire to build something useful, recognition and prize money were certainly welcome.

In addition, the competition gave Elizabeth's team the legitimacy it needed to recruit big name institutions to beta test their app. Elizabeth connected with Matt Peron through the competition website, and he introduced her to additional organizations that could help beta test. Without his influence, it's unlikely she would have connected with these other organizations as easily.

3. Improve government transparency by making open data accessible

The data Elizabeth's team used was all freely available, it just wasn't being used. Most people are not able to locate relevant information in a giant spreadsheet quickly and easily. iFinditChicago.com made city government more transparent by providing an easy way to find and use information about city services.

In the future, this transparent data can be used to keep governments accountable. For example, now that citizens have an easy way to analyze the distribution of food banks, they can push for more local food choices. Mashed together with demographic data, the public also could demonstrate areas where social services are under-served.

Government Efficiency

4. Create apps that benefit people and businesses

Governor Pat Quinn deemed iFinditChicago.com so useful that he asked Elizabeth's team to build iFinditIllinois.com so people and institutions across the state could use it also.

It's too soon to know whether or not iFinditChicago.com will last, but we do know that Illinois has moved forward with a state level version, and an institution in San Francisco is planning on building a similar app. Even though most competition apps don't long outlast the awards ceremony, they can lend credence to the benefits of open government data

Even if the original iFinditChicago.com app falls into disuse, it has already helped people, institutions and businesses by providing a tangible demonstration of open data apps.

5. Crowdsource public data priorities

Governments collect millions of lines of data, but publishing resources are limited. Developers interested in entering CACs can have great ideas for apps, and then find that the data set they need isn't available. CACs create a clear channel for communicating data priorities, which organizers will experience as soon as the data request emails start rolling in.

Because Elizabeth looked to the data first and built on what she found, her case doesn't illustrate this benefit. However, during the competition we received dozens of requests for data sets that were not yet public. We passed them on to Chicago's CDO; there's the opportunity for him to use the "wish list" to prioritize the publishing of new data.

Economic Growth

6. Drive innovation

Innovation is all about solving tricky problems in new ways. IFinditChicago solved a problem for the public sector; other apps used open data to create for-profit apps. The most famous one from Chicago is perhaps SpotHero, an app that connects people who need parking spaces with people who have them. SpotHero was accepted into Excelerate Labs, a local start-up accelerator, in 2012. But as yet and as discussed above, an energetic level of private sector activity with open civic data as its fuel has yet to be experienced. Everyone is waiting for the "civic" equivalent of private sector innovation that has come about because of federal data; for example, BrightScope, built with 401(k) reports from the Bureau of Labor Statistics, or The Weather Channel, built with satellite data from the National Weather Service.

7. Build a community of practice around open government data

We can't stress enough how building a community of practice around open government data is one of the most important reasons for a CAC.

For example, what's most notable about Elizabeth's experience is the sheer number of people, companies, governments and non-profits she connected with in the course of building her app. We've mapped them out here in Figure 2-1.

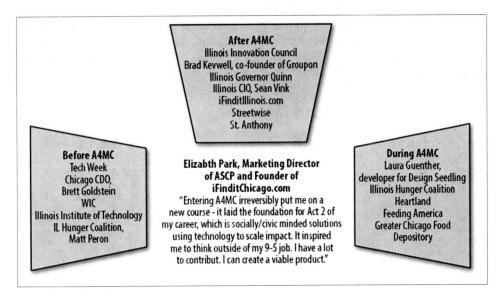

Figure 2-1. Elizabeth Park as community hub

There isn't a marketing campaign in the world that could have created this network. It took a competition to inspire Elizabeth to reach out to all these different people and groups.

Today Elizabeth, along with dozens of other A4MC participants, remains deeply engaged with the Chicago open government data and technology community. She was most recently invited to speak at Chicago DataDive, a hackathon designed to connect developers with non-profits in need of data help.

Apps for Metro Chicago transformed Elizabeth from someone vaguely interested in technology to an active and engaged participant in projects and communities built around open government data.

Our experience with A4MC and Clay Johnson's perspective noted above is becoming perhaps the most important theme in the open government data community. Alexander Howard reports on a spate of similar opinion from open data evangelists, technologists, journalists and private sector entrepreneurs in 2011.[1] He quotes a White House "Champion of Change", Waldo Jacquith: "There isn't an inherent problem in app contests, I don't think, but they're probably not worth bothering with unless there's a

---

1. "Everyone jumped on the app contest bandwagon. Now what?" *http://radar.oreilly.com/2011/08/app-contests-sustainability-usability.html*

simultaneous effort to foster a community around those data." Speaking to the usefulness of jus the apps themselves, Anthony Townsend, Research Director at the Institute for the Future, recently tweeted "[Health apps are awful] but might as well be [said] about city data contest apps too."[2]

Next Chapter: Goals and Metrics

Benefits are all well and good, but in our next chapter we translate them into goals and metrics.

2. July 11, 2012, @anthonymobile

CHAPTER 3

Identifying Goals and Metrics for Your Apps Competition

Why are you holding a civic apps competition? What are you trying to achieve? These are important questions, because the goals you identify for your competition will direct every aspect of the design and planning process.

A review of 15 civic apps competitions shows remarkable consistency in the stated goals; organizers wanted to improve transparency, cut government costs, benefit people and businesses, and drive innovation.

While these goals are a good starting point, they are vaguely defined and difficult to measure. In addition, they don't capture any of the benefits of building a community of developers, businesses, and institutions interested in using open government data.

This is a short chapter where we're going to tease out how to measure benefits of civic apps competitions that we covered in Chapter 2. This discussion might help you decide among goals, or prioritize them. At the end of the chapter we've included a table pairing each goal with a range of metrics, so if text isn't your bag skip to Table 3-1.

Translating Benefits into Goals and Metrics

1. Raise Awareness of Available Open Government Data Sources

"Raising awareness" is a communications term that means getting the word out to the public about an issue. Traditionally this is measured by the number of media hits the issue receives.

For a CAC, raising awareness means to inspire as many people as possible to participate in the competition. So in addition to pursuing coverage of the competition in the news media, CAC organizers can segment their audience and develop a communication strategy tailored to each group.

For example, all CAC organizers want to engage developers. Working through local meet-ups, listservs, and tech stars is a much more effective way to reach developers than getting a story in the local daily paper. Tracking the number of threads, tweets and meet-ups is a more robust way to measure awareness in your target community.

2. Build Apps on Open Data

The key to this goal is quantity of apps, not quality. Generating a large pool of submitted apps is the raison d'être of a CAC, and it's a robust way to measure engagement with the competition data. After all, even a poorly designed app is the result of hours of work from a developer engaging with the competition data.

Participation in competition events such as hackathons, brainstorming sessions, and meetings with community leaders can be a secondary metric to measure efforts at building apps on open data. A developer who spends a day working with competition data is engaged with app building, even if she doesn't ultimately submit an application to the competition.

3. Create Apps That Benefit Residents, Visitors, and Businesses

CACs tend to receive many submissions for apps that do neat, but not necessarily useful, stuff. My favorite example of this is "NY Party," a game app that puts you on a quest to buy three hotdogs in different neighborhoods. Fun? Sure! Useful? Only if you're Takeru Kobayashi, champion competitive eater.

The most direct way to measure the usefulness of an app is to track the number of times it is downloaded. Unfortunately, this metric is less robust in a competition setting because CAC sites or the app's developers aren't connected to popular app shopping sites like the Apple Store. This makes the competition apps difficult for casual users to find, which makes it difficult for even amazing and useful apps to find an audience.

There are three ways to indirectly measure the usefulness of an app. The first is to track the number of apps built based on an idea contributed to the competition. The CAC site can host an app suggestion page and solicit ideas from the public. In this scenario, an app built in response to a specific request can safely be considered useful to at least one person—the requestor!

The second is to track the number of apps built in collaboration with an institution or business. When an organization participates in a CAC, it's usually because they hope the finished app can improve their business or service.

The third way is to let the judges decide which apps are most useful to the community. This method has the added benefit of allowing a judgment call in the absence of apps built by suggestion or in collaboration.

Using a combination of two or more of these metrics provides a more nuanced picture of the usefulness of the apps created.

4. Improve Government Transparency

CACs improve government transparency by motivating developers to build apps that make it easy for people to use civic data. The most direct way to translate that benefit into a goal is to track the number of different data sets used by competing developers. Every data set made usable by an app is a win for transparency.

CACs also improve transparency by identifying flaws in government data sets. Governments want to publish data that is usable to the developer community, but developers frequently find bugs or errors when working with these data sets. Every time a developer reports a data flaw, the government has more grassroots information about how their transparency efforts are working. CACs can help you track both data flaws, and the rate at which they are addressed, providing your organization two additional transparency metrics.

A CAC could also host a platform that app developers use to request particular data sets (discussed below). If the government responds to a request by creating access to new data, transparency has been improved.

5. Drive Innovation

In Chapter 1 we defined innovation in a CAC competition as "a new solution to a problem." There are two ways to measure the long-term adoption rates of apps over the length of a competition: tracking the number of apps spun out into a business, and tracking the number of apps folded into governments and institutions. This is a measure that might take a while to track—some apps, for example, won't be embraced immediately and will take longer than the length of the competition to fully develop.

6. Crowdsource Data Publishing Priorities

CACs can be an effective way to crowdsource data priorities, because participating developers or community organizations discover that the data set they need to build out their app isn't available.

How effective is your CAC is at crowdsourcing data priorities? The most direct way to measure is to track the number of data requests that emerge from your competition. You can develop a more complete metric by including whether or not those requests change the government's data publishing schedule.

7. Build a Community of Practice Around Open Government Data

The most valuable outcome of a CAC is that it helps build a community of practice around open government data by fostering new relationships between experts in different fields. Developers, entrepreneurs, NGO workers, government officials, and interested citizens can all participate and build relationships based on a mutual interest in government data.

Unfortunately, there is no direct way to measure community building. Some participants will engage with civic data, others will decide to walk away. In addition, the benefits of these new relationships and new ideas keep accruing long after the CAC is over and tangible outcomes like new businesses or policy approaches rarely happen within the scope of the competition.

The best way to manage this ambiguity is to track the actions taken by CAC participants. How many businesses held events connected with the competition? How many developers attended one or more hacking sessions? How many NGO's partnered with a developer to build an app? Mapping out these connections can give an idea of how successful the CAC was in building bridges between different groups. We mapped those connections in two ways.

The first, in Figure 3-1, is a traditional conversion funnel. This map gives the viewer a sense of how much work goes into recruiting competition submissions.

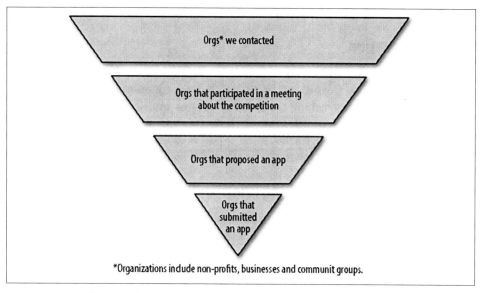

Figure 3-1. Traditional "conversion funnel" visualization of apps competition outcomes

The second, in Figure 3-2, is a participation map, which shows all the ways people and organizations participated, not just by submitting apps.

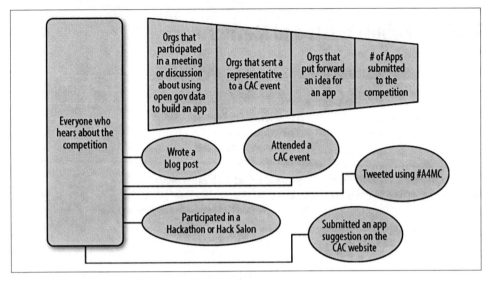

Figure 3-2. Measuring total CAC participation

Identifying Your Competition's Ideal Goals and Metrics of Success

Now that you understand how different goals will play out in an apps competition, you can identify the ones that are important to your organization. Next, you will use this information to develop a plan, building in ample learning steps to analyze your success metrics.

Apps competitions can be designed to achieve different outcomes, so your selection of goals will structure your overall strategy. For example, a competition that strives to maximize the number of submissions would be structured very differently from a competition designed to maximize partnerships between developers and community institutions.

A case in point is NYCBigApps, which has organized three civic apps competitions. The first two encouraged developers to create useful apps with the city's data. The third iteration was a little different. This time, the organizers decided to maximize the number of ideas by encouraging a more general participation. They wanted to get more people involved who could identify problems that could be solved with city data—whether or not they had the developer skills to build out apps.

In order to meet this new goal, New York held a pre-competition strictly to solicit ideas for apps from the public. Over 600 entries were submitted in the ideas round—nearly six times as many entries as the first NYC BigApps competition.

Table of Robust Goals and Metrics

Table 3-1. Robust goals and metrics for Civic Apps Competitions

Goals	Metrics
1a: Raising awareness of available government data in the developer community	# of hits on competition data sets # of events held by developers # of tweets from local tech stars # of apps submitted
1b: Raising awareness of mission relevant open government data in the non-profit community	# of requests for data sets from non-profits # of apps submitted in partnership with non-profits Diversity of the map of engaged community organizations
1c: Raising awareness of open government data availability in the general public	# of press hits # of public votes
2. Build apps on open data	Total # of apps submitted Total participation in CAC hacking events
3. Create apps that benefit residents, visitors and businesses.	# of apps built in response to requests from organizations # of apps built in collaboration with an institution or business CAC judge assessments
4. Improve government transparency	# of data sets used by applicants # of flaws identified in government data sets # of flaws fixed
5. Drive innovation	# of competition apps spun out into a business # of apps integrated into an existing institution or business # of apps in use beyond a year # of downloads
6. Crowdsource data priorities	# of new data requests from businesses and community organizations # of data sets moved to a higher priority release date due to popular demand
7a. Build a community of practice: linking developers and community organizations	# of apps built in collaboration between developers and community organizations
7b. Build a community of practice: linking developers and government	# of apps built in collaboration between developers and government # of visits to government data catalogues # of flaws identified and fixed in the government data
7c. Build a community of practice: local businesses and developers	# of businesses that hosted or contributed meaningful support to hacking events
7d. Build a community of practice: number of developers participating in the competition	# of developers that attended at least one event # of developers that attended multiple events, even if they didn't submit an app # of unsolicited blog posts and tweets about the CAC

Next Chapter: Building Your Budget

Before finalizing the CAC's goals, organizers should conduct a survey of the resources available to support the competition. In the next chapter, we cover that most important of resources: the budget.

CHAPTER 4

Building Your CAC Budget

Few CACs make their revenues and expenses transparent. The only CAC we could find that published any budget numbers was Washington DC's Apps for Democracy, which reported an expense of $50,000. But that number reflects a one-time payment to iStrategyLabs to run the competition. Each NYCBig Apps is about $100,000 all-inclusive, but a breakout by task isn't available.

We're going sidestep this lack of precedent in two ways: by walking you through the priciest components of a CAC (cash prizes, web platform, administrative support, technical support and competition length); and by publishing for the first time ever what the Metro Chicago Information Center (MCIC) spent on running the Apps for Metro Chicago competition (A4MC) in 2011. Keeping these costs in mind will help you design a competition that fits your budget. We'll also explore the ways that partners and sponsors can reduce your costs.

Partners

Most CACs require partnerships, and for the discussion below to make sense, we should describe a typical competition's partners—there are five kinds. First, if the City or other government agency isn't running the competition itself, there's likely to be a *managing* partner—for us, that was MCIC. The city and other government suppliers of data are *data* partners. Then there are *funding* partners who put up prize money and fund administration of the competition. *Sponsorship* partners donate time, space or money for events, give in-kind contributions such as testing devices, or in-kind prizes such as cloud services for winners. An important subset of sponsorship partners are *apps sponsors*. These are organizations that are interested in supporting the development of a particular kind of app. For example, in A4MC the Delta Institute sponsored the development of a "green app" by putting up a bit of prize money and sponsoring a hack day.

The Data

Governments collect data in a variety of ways, and sadly the data sets are stored in a variety of ways too. Since developers need clean, structured data to build apps (more on this in the next chapter), you may have to undertake a data clean-up as the first step in the competition. If resources for data development need to be taken into account, that will take a bite out of the competition budget. Depending on your level of readiness, these costs can range from the tens of thousands to the hundreds of thousands. Apps for Metro Chicago benefited from already-structured data sitting on RESTful web servers that had been developed over the course of 18 months before the CAC was announced. While the city government declined to provide information about the cost of preparing the initial 70 data sets that we used to start the competition, we estimate the cost to the city at roughly $100,000.

Cash Prizes

Over the past three years, award amounts have grown by leaps and bounds. The biggest prize pool we found clocked in at $100,000 for 2011's Apps for Communities, which was run by the Knight Foundation and the Federal Communications Commission. Apps for Metro Chicago's final bill for cash prizes was about $65,000, including the original amount set aside by the City of Chicago, as well as add-on prizes for apps sponsored by specific organizations.

But we have good news for organizers without that kind of money: a review of 15 North American CACs shows no relationship between the number of entries and the size of the prize money pool (Figure 4-1).

Notice that five CACs offering less prize money attracted more submissions than Apps for Communities; and the EPA's Apps for the Environment collected 38 entries despite offering no cash at all.

We still recommend offering cash prizes, but the jury is out on whether or not it's the best to splurge. Although they remain an important incentive, it looks like there are diminishing returns at some point. However, Tom Lee at Sunlight Labs maintains that prizes were "vital to Sunlight's Civic Apps Competitions."[1]

1. Personal communication, July 2012.

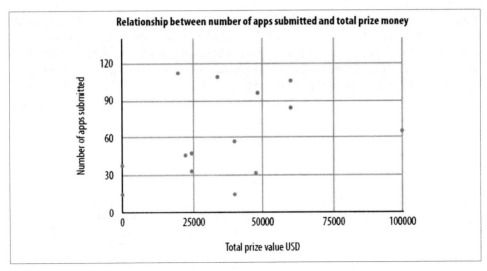

Figure 4-1. Relationship between number of apps submitted and prize amount

Competition Web Platform

All competitions require a web-based platform to share information about the competition, allow developers to submit their apps, and possibly run a public voting process. Competition organizers have two choices: build a one-off competition website, or work with an established vendor like ChallengePost, Skild, or NetSquared. These vendors offer anything from simply hosting a competition website to designing the entire effort, recruiting applicants, drafting rules, and distributing prizes.

Given the lack of transparency about competition budgets to date, it is difficult to conduct a thorough cost-benefit analysis of hiring a vendor or building a one-off website. Nevertheless, there are a number of factors that every organizer should consider:

- Is there anyone in-house who can build a site with all the features you need?
- How long would it take your staff to build and maintain that site?
- How much do you have to spend?
- Are you planning to host future competitions, or is this competition a one-time event?

It is very easy to underestimate the cost of building a one-off site capable of hosting comments, managing app submissions, and handling public voting. For example, A4MC hired a contractor to build a standalone competition site using free open source software and the bill still exceeded $60,000. If you don't have the internal expertise to build a site, you should strongly consider hiring a vendor. Table 4-1 is meant to be a handy guide to help you decide whether you should build a one-off or not.

Keep in mind that, whether you build it in-house or out, the cost of additional features rarely makes them worth it. A4MC included a "conversation" area where we encouraged developers and community groups to do matchmaking, but in reality that's a function that we really needed to do in person (see more below). A developer conversation area was similarly little-used. Stick to the basics—the platform really only needs to explain the rules and regulations of the contest, host submitted apps, and handle public voting.

Table 4-1. Building a one-off vs. hiring a vendor

	Pros	Cons	Recommended for
Custom platform	• Use existing staff resources • Design exactly what you need	• The cost may rise unexpectedly • Big time commitment	• Simple sites with no comments or public voting • Organizers with in-house expertise • Competitions planned as an annual event
Vendor platform	• Use existing staff resources • Design exactly what you need • Price clarity: Vendors can give you the price up front, no overrun costs • Buying expertise from people who have built competition websites before • Low time commitment	• High upfront price • Less control	• Complex sites with comments, public voting and other interactive features • One-off competitions • Organizers with limited time and strict budgets

Administration

Running even a simple CAC requires a lot of behind-the-scenes work and it's important to budget enough staff to manage it. Because staffing varies so widely across offices, we're breaking out the administrative tasks necessary for running a CAC, as well as providing a list of roles. The list may feel overwhelming, but as they say the devil's in the details. In our experience the cost is in the details, too.

Project Director

The role of the project director is to conceptualize the competition, get the project started, make the initial connections among partners and sponsors, set up the "rules of the road," and direct high-level traffic. The project director might be the same person as the project manager (described next), but if that's the case, realize that this person will need to juggle air-traffic control, along with day-to-day ground support and maintenance throughout the competition. MCIC spent $35,000 on such high-level tasks which include:

- Setting the frame
- Generating internal support
- Designing competition structure
- Establishing competition goals and design
- Designing rules, timing and prize categories
- Creating budget(s) and partnership agreements
- Identifying key players
- Recruiting partners and/or sponsors
- Finding prize money and sponsorships
- Identifying and recruit judges
- Leading the partnership
- Resolving conflicts
- Taking calls from organizational and community leaders
- Making major decisions on strategy and direction

Project Manager

The project manager is in control of day-to-day operations. The list of tasks below represents a potentially incredible amount of work and attention to detail, depending on the complexity of the competition design and the number of partners. MCIC spent $75,000 on project management for A4MC for the following tasks:

- Develop the project timeline, meeting schedule, and keep everyone on task
- Develop and spearhead outreach plans to community organizations and software developers
- Develop the rules and regulations, undertake a legal review
- Coordinate external partners
- Field calls and develop relationships with partners and sponsors
- Plan for coordinated marketing and outreach and media strategy
- Vendors and events
- Find venues and participants for events
- Organize hackathons
- Organize prize award ceremonies
- Oversee judging
- Develop judging rubric and ensure compliance

- Cajole and track judges and oversee judging process
- Obtain platforms for judges to enable them to evaluate the apps
- Oversee vote tallying and identify potential issues to check for cheaters
- Coordinate internal communications, event, legal and competition website staff

Outreach and Coordination to Civic Organizations and Civic Hackers

One of the main themes of the Apps for Metro Chicago competition was to emphasize community outreach in a way perhaps not done before. Our intention was to generate apps that addressed important issues by Chicago area residents; because community organizations deal with these issues, they are best situated to understand the dynamic needs of their communities. Ideally this outreach would result in apps which are just not technologically innovative, but helpful for the day to day lives of Chicago residents—and that because the apps generated met community needs, they would be more likely to have longevity.

We set up a Google Group to facilitate matchmaking. We'd hoped that community organizations would go to the Google Group themselves, seek out a partner, and only need our help for data questions and getting started. But this was a high expectation. Instead, we took on the task of publishing their ideas to the Google Group and directing any responses back to them. We then called them, scheduled a brainstorming session, gathered ideas, and matched them with a developer. Negotiating trust, overcoming the technical language barrier and facilitating the relationship was fairly complex. This outreach and match-making contributed about $20,000 to the costs of project management.

Communications

Unless done by the project manager, the role of a communications specialist is to coordinate media and outreach. The more partners and the more rounds of competition, the larger the budget. The communications director's task is also made more difficult when trying to reach multiple audiences and participants: community groups, developers, artist communities, etc. The A4MC budget was about $75,000 for tasks such as:

- Developing press and social media strategy
- Creating content for social media channels
- Organizing events

Technical Support

The role of technical support is to manage internal technical issues around the competition and respond to developer requests and questions. For A4MC, we included technical assistance on the metadata, and review of the use of the data in the app itself. We spent $55,000 on technical support:

- Build and/or manage the competition website
- Answer developer questions about data
- Escalate information about bugs and data errors to the data partners
- Screen app submissions for functionality and adherence to competition rules
- Support judges during the app judging process
- Monitor public voting for cheating

Legal Review

The managing partner should have a lawyer available to review the rules of the competition and protect the partners from liability.

- Ensure the competition rules are in compliance with the law
- Protect the organizers from liability
- Protect the partners from liability

Not all competitions are complicated enough to require all these tasks, but even the simplest competition takes serious time and effort to pull off. Be realistic in your assessment of the working hours needed to accomplish administrative tasks and design your competition accordingly. A shorter, simpler competition that runs well is far preferable to a long, complex competition that annoys all the organizers and participants. Given the number of partners and the complexity of relationships, legal review cost A4MC $25,000.

The legal version of our rules and regulations are available at www.urbanrubrics.com.

Technical Support

There are two kinds of of technical support you may decide to include in your CAC: managing the competition website, and answering developers' questions about the data. We touched on the need to have someone manage the competition website above, so here we will focus on what we believe was one of the distinctive characteristics of A4MC: cleaning competition data and answering questions about it.

One of the great truths of life is that developers will find errors in the course of working with data, no matter how stringently it's cleaned beforehand. They will attempt to report them to you and will be annoyed if they are ignored.

A simple way to manage questions and complaints is to set up a ticket-based support system like Zendesk or osTicket. These systems collect questions and error reports from developers and direct them to support staff. Once the questions are answered they can be posted on the competition site for other developers to access.

Most competitions do not provide competing developers with systematic technical support, but it is a good way to improve the quality of both the raw data and the competition apps.

Competition Length

The CACs we surveyed ranged from 1 to 7 months in length, but, as Figure 4-2 shows, adding extra time after the 4 month mark doesn't have much effect on the quantity of apps submitted.

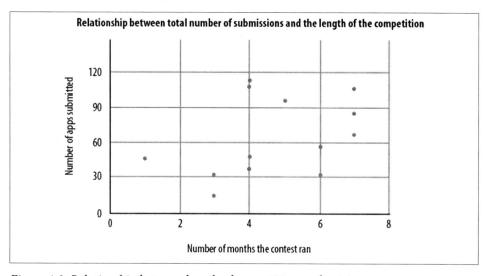

Figure 4-2. Relationship between length of competition and entries

Of course, we don't know if the length of the competition has an effect on the quality of the apps. We're inclined to think that quality is influenced more by good communications, networking and hackathons than the number of months the competition runs. So if you have to trim the budget somewhere, we recommend shortening the competition.

Additional Costs

Other costs that you may need to budget for include:

Support for the judges
> Judges need smartphones upon which to judge the apps, will have questions for the technical staff, etc. Be sure to ask yourself "Where will these smartphones come from?"

The time/cost of finding venues for and coordinating events
> This takes much longer than one might think. The cost for this to A4MC was about $20,000.

Managing post-contest complaints
> A4MC fielded complaints from developers who didn't win, some of whom challenged the legality of particular apps.

Defraying Costs

After that list of competition expenses you're probably just about ready to hurl this book across the room. Before you do, think about whether or not you can recruit partners or sponsors to help defray the costs. Many of the apps competition we reviewed had partners and sponsors. Canada's Apps 4 Climate teamed up with Microsoft, SAP, Telus, Netscribe, Analytic Design Group, eaves.ca, Harbour Air Seaplanes, and the Vancouver Aquarium. And that wasn't even the competition with the most partners and sponsors—that honor goes to Portland's Civic Apps, which clocked in at a whopping 16 partners and sponsors.

The downside of recruiting partners is that you lose some control over the structure of the competition. For example, A4MC was funded largely by the MacArthur Foundation and the Chicago Community Trust, two foundations that support non-profits and charitable causes. As a result, the competing developers were required to make their apps free to the public for a year instead of being able to bring them to market. We found that this put off a number of would-be competitors.

Usually the upsides to partnering more than make up for the drawbacks—and not just for the funding. Apps for Metro Chicago was able to leverage the CCT and MacArthur networks to engage non-profits and other civic institutions in the competition.

Partners and Workload

An important lesson we learned in terms of administration is that the administrative resources you will need to devote to these tasks tend to *increase exponentially as more partners come on board*. Having more partners is a fabulous thing—whether they are app sponsors, data providers (A4MC had data from the state, the county, the city and the local regional planning agency), or other backers. A variety and large number of partners can be a boon to the competition terms of the apps that can be built and the buzz generated. However, each partner adds another dimension to the social media strategy, coordination efforts, input-to-be-obtained-from, etc. We took at least one late-night call from a partner unhappy about the placement of their logo on the competition website. Partners are great, but they're a double-edged sword.

Also, not all partners are equal in their ability to take on their required tasks (such as developing marketing and outreach for their sponsored app). When entering into partnerships, be sure to structure the relationship so that it truly fits the task at hand and the available resources. What we learned is that expectations needed to be made explicit. Assumptions about the ability to piggyback on existing capacity can lead to a fraught relationship and unrealistic expectations. Organizations that want to sponsor an app, for example, might not have the ability to do a media roll-out and might need help from the managing partner to do that.

The largest two items that contributed to administrative costs are apt to be the number of competition rounds and the number of partners. This presents a conundrum: more rounds create more excitement and engagement and potential for good apps, but they come at a price.

More partners also means more data and more possibilities for cross-fertilization, but again, this creates a greater workload for the managing partner.

Next Chapter: Data Resources

A budget is necessary, but the really critical resource for a terrific competition is a good data selection. In the next chapter we walk you through everything you need to know to assess your data resources.

CHAPTER 5

Surveying Your Data Resources

Data is the star of the competition, so it's a natural instinct to publish everything you can. However, you will get better developer buy-in and better apps if you are selective in choosing your competition's data sets.

In this chapter we cover three questions you can expect to hear from the developers participating in your competition:

- How is the data structured?
- What is the content?
- What is the documentation?

We'll also address the importance of providing technical support.

Structured Versus Unstructured Data

As you determine the data that will be used in your apps competition, first consider its format. While you may have a lot of data available, it may not be in the correct format to fuel apps.

Structured data resides in fixed fields, as in a database, and is available in a machine readable format. Software developers that all government data be structured.

Unfortunately, most governments store data in paper or digital systems, which are referred to by data programmers as *unstructured*. Unstructured data includes information in legacy systems such as paper forms, word processing files, magnetic tapes, microfiche, card files, floppy disks, etc.

While valuable and essential for many government operations, unstructured data is not a good platform for an apps competition for several reasons. First, it raises entry barriers for programmers who must first convert the data into a structured format before they can build their app, conduct their analysis or construct their vision. The process of data transformation is time-consuming and significantly increases the risk of misused data. Converting data can also require skill sets beyond the scope of developers, like performing data analysis, normalization and standardization. If poorly handled, different apps could reach different conclusions from the same data, which would confuse users.

While relying only on structured data for your competition is ideal, the reality is that storing and publishing data in structured formats is still a relatively new practice in government.

It is no coincidence that Apps for Democracy was borne out of Washington D.C.'s expansive CapStat project, which was among the first in the nation to share structured, real-time government data feeds and had the largest open data catalog of any city, worldwide. Access to structured data made it easy for D.C.'s small but active technology community to start building, so a project to encourage innovative uses of the data was a logical next step.

Once you have identified the data you want to use, you will need to make it available to participating developers. The most advanced way is to make your structured data available through web services by using on an open Application Programming Interface (API) via a web HTTP protocol. Such API interfaces allow real-time mashups with other structured data and drive the development of mobile apps. Many of the partners in the A4MC competition used the Socrata platform built for local governments (*http://www.socrata.com/*).

All that being the case, there may be room in your competition for encouraging the development of structured data itself as part of or an outcome of the competition. A4MC and other competitions have been fortunate to have a CTO or a CIO who had already made government data structured and available through an API. Places with less structured data or who have not decided on the right API investment should not be dissuaded.

Allowing bulk data downloads (as opposed to live API feeds) is "good enough" to kick start a competition, especially if one of the competition goals is to create a community of users. Bonding over "what does this data really say" is a good way to get community advocates and software developers in a room together.

In addition, if a goal of a CAC is to improve government transparency by making open government data available, then by all means having developers and analysts scrub and otherwise wrangle with the unstructured data is to be encouraged. But there then has to be a way for the clean data to be made public. A4MC wasn't set up to do this—in fact one of our requirements was that the apps had to use one of the live data feeds. But we see no reason why there might not be room for a "Civic *Data* Competition" where the return to the government entity and public is clean data. Below we profile an organization called DataKind whose goal is just this for entities in the social sector.

Data Content

Not all government data is created equal. While governments collect and possess many different kinds of data that can be useful for achieving Open Government Data goals, you need the right mix of data in order to energize a CAC. What kind of data works?

It might be helpful to think of government data as of kinds: organizational data, and government operations data.

Organizational Data

Organizational data describes the structure of a government entity, and the political process of development policies, programs and legislation. This would include staff salaries, meeting minutes, lobbyist records, budgets, procurement records, FOIA requests etc. Operational data illustrates how the government is structured and how it makes decisions.

This type of data is especially useful when the goal is to engage citizens around issues of accountability. Operational data can be used for creating interactive budgets, tracking lobbying activity, constructing searchable city council meeting minutes: Apps that meet the goals of transparency, citizen engagement and government accountability. These are items that might not be top picks at your local apps store, but they lead to fabulous insights which address the open government data goal of government accountability.

Government Operations

Operations data is information about the services governments perform and where they perform them. It's fairly dynamic data in that it can reflect real-time performance (e.g., bus arrival estimates). Since the data can change on an hourly or daily basis, it's the juice that most encourages app development for smartphones: sanitation, street closures, emergency dispatch, food pantries, bus and train routes and delays, restaurant inspections, traffic camera locations, curb cuts, etc.

Think of all the data collected by city departments as they go about their business: information about compliance and regulations (business permits, housing code violations, property transfers, etc.); participation levels in government-sponsored programs (health care clinics, after-school programs), infrastructure maintenance and development (filling potholes, installing traffic lights, landscaping parks), public safety and health (911 and 311 calls, crime records, vermin abatement).

It's a gold mine. The more of this kind of data you can make available, the better apps you'll get in return.

Even before the advent of ever-present web platforms and smartphones, government efficiency specialists used this data extensively to understand government performance and to develop real-time performance measures about city operations. These "performance dashboards" were made public. For example, launched in the late 1990s, Baltimore's *Citistat* program was one of the first broadly-implemented programs of this kind. St. Petersburg, Fl. implemented *City Scorecard* in the early 2000s.

These early performance indicator initiatives helped lay the groundwork for today's open government data movement and associated CACs. As web capacity increased in the last decade, the data used to create the performance indicators moved to "web enabled data sharing"—not just prefabricated indicators, but the raw data itself. Now, rather than (or in addition to) creating their own performance indicators, cities and counties are able to publish the raw data and invite the public to create performance indicators as well as other, more dynamic, apps. Now, current data about government operations is the basis for most apps.

Data on operations is most often coupled with GIS boundary files (property borders, precinct delineations, tax increment districts, zoning corridors, hydrology, census tract boundaries, etc.) to create the smartest place-based apps. Boundary files not only allow software developers to construct apps that can let citizens know where government services are taking place, but also allow citizen reporting. For example, a fairly common app for cities now is one that allows citizens to report the condition of their neighborhood streets and sidewalks and pinpoint streets that need to be plowed, potholes that need to be filled, hydrants that aren't working, and more.

Documentation

Just as it is important to share the right data in the right format, it is also vital that governments share detailed information about what the data means, and how it was collected. This information is referred to as "metadata"—data about data. Metadata provides the context that makes it possible for analysts and developers to draw accurate conclusions.

Consider, for example, the possible data that is generated by a municipality for a single pothole:

1. A resident calls 311 to report that a pothole at the 100 block of Main Street; the operator creates a ticket number for this call.

2. Public Works is notified and the ticket is assigned to a crew.

3. The Public Works supervisor adds a number of fields to the data about this single pothole: the date and time it was assigned, the number of the truck assigned, the expected date it will be filled.

4. As the Public Works crew fixes the pothole, they walk up and down the 100 block of Main to check for other unreported potholes or problems.

5. They spot an additional pothole and a broken manhole cover and fix both, noting their activities on a clipboard.

6. The crew returns to the garage and files a report on both the assigned pothole, as well as the additional work performed.

7. When data from that report is entered, the original pothole ticket is marked as "closed," with a date and time stamp. The additional work performed by the crew is noted in a separate "other problems completed" log.

This describes a fairly common scenario in government operations, and demonstrates how data is capture in multiple ways for a single activity: citizen reporting, operational processes, and actual on-the-street activity. These reports may never find themselves in the same dataset, but if the municipality published just part of the data, or published without clear and comprehensive metadata, it would lead to performance measures that could be misleading.

Consider this: Without knowledge of the "other problems completed" log, an analyst or software developer might conclude that the ratio of potholes filled to hours worked suggests inefficiencies at best, or worse, graft. Without documentation explaining that citizen data on potholes, and crew data on additional work could be stored in different data sets, the public might never link sets to present a comprehensive picture of Public Works activities.

Unfortunately metadata development is time-consuming and expensive; consequently government data sharing efforts are light on documentation. What is needed is both a description of the data set, as well as documentation for every each variable in the set (historically called a data dictionary). A way to solve this for a particular CAC is to have either data curation help (MCIC played this role for A4MC), or to have a subject-matter expert from the sponsoring agency(ies) available for consultation.

Your time is best spent on documenting data that will be released, rather than releasing a larger quantity of data. An additional approach is to make someone from the department that produced the data available at hackathons and other COC events.

In Chapter 4, we identified technical support as one of the most expensive elements of a CAC, but it's also one of the best ways to maximize the impact of your competition. Fixing errors in the data and building out good data dictionaries demonstrates that you understand developer's needs. It makes it easier for them to enter the CAC, and improves the quality of submitted apps. As an added bonus, once a data set is cleaned, it's in better working condition long after the competition ends.

Next Chapter: Design

Now that you've dutifully covered all the nuts and bolts of creating a CAC it's time for the fun part: design!

CHAPTER 6

Designing Your CAC

Now that you've identified your goals, estimated a budget, reviewed your data resources and assessed your political support, it's time for the fun part: designing your competition!

In this chapter we walk you through all the elements of a CAC that you can shape to create the outcomes you want: the participation incentives, prize categories, judging criteria, judging process, judge selection, eligible apps and events and communications. The legal version of the rules and regulations we discuss below can be found at www.urbanrubrics.com.

Participation Incentives

Cash is a popular incentive for driving participation, and with good reason. Everyone likes winning money, and it makes a terrific hook for media coverage. However, developers decide to participate in a competition for a range of reasons. Socrata's Open Government Data Benchmark Study found that developers were primarily motivated by the desire to have an impact on people's lives, their interest in the challenge and their personal commitment to open data.[1] Just 2.5% identified profitability as their primary motivator, which makes sense when you consider that building an app is expensive and in a competition there is no guarantee of any return.

This is good news for CAC organizers because it opens up a wide range of incentives apart from cash, such as those explained in the next few sections.

---

1. Open Government Data Benchmark Study, Socrata *http://www.socrata.com/benchmark-study/*

Multiple Award Categories

For developers and people who want to hire them, projects are more important than degrees. Building a prize winning app demonstrates a skill set better than a resume ever could.

This also holds true for companies who sell their services as apps builders. All three winning entries in the EPA's Apps for the Environment were submitted by app development companies, and all three advertise their wins on the company homepage.

CAC organizers can support this motivation by creating multiple award categories. Naming 10 winners for 10 separate categories creates more glory than naming the top ten winners in a single category. It sounds much better to be the winner of the health app category than to be the ninth place runner-up overall.

Professional Networking Opportunities

Having a personal connection with a company is one of the best ways to get a job, and a CAC offers a good platform for targeted networking. There are two ways to organize professional networking incentives for a CAC: as an incentive for developers to participate during the course of the competition, or as a reward for winners at the end of the competition. What we also did was to emphasize the use of judges who were local and could thus be around in the longer term for formal or informal mentorship.

The Apps for Metro Chicago Competition offered both types. During the competition, Google's Chicago offices hosted two city data hackathons. Everyone wants to work at Google, so developers swarmed both events. Several of the apps submitted to the competition got their start at those hackathons.

After the competition, winners were invited to present their work to the Chicago Council for Innovation. As a result, the winners met with some of the most famous names in Chicago's technology field, including Brad Keywell, co-founder of Groupon, and Matt Maloney, co-founder and CEO of GrubHub.

Both the Google-hosted hackathons and the presentation to the CCI created ways for developers to meet influential people in their field through participation in the competition. And as an added bonus, they didn't cost the CAC organizers anything but their time.

Solving an Interesting Problem

As in any profession, developers are hired to work on projects that make money rather than projects they find interesting. CACs present an opportunity to work with new data and to solve new problems.

CAC organizers can support this motivation by actively working to connect developers with organizations or government departments that have problems that need solving.

Prize Categories

Prize categories are one of the most powerful ways to nudge developers to focus on specific topics. Competitors look to prize categories for insight into the kinds of apps likely to win. For example, setting separate prizes for web and mobile apps will nudge developers to work in diverse formats. Offering separate awards by themes like transportation and health will encourage developers to focus on those subject areas.

As we discussed in Chapter 5, data availability is another key consideration when setting your prize categories. If the majority of your data consists of information about parking and transportation issues, creating a prize for the best crime app isn't going to have much influence on the submissions.

Judging Criteria

Judging criteria also have a powerful influence. There are two approaches to judging rules: open-ended or targeted.

The Open-Ended Approach

Organizers using the open-ended approach provide vague terms like "innovative," "creative," "useful," and "valuable" as judging criteria. Their goal is to attract as many developers to participate as possible, both by setting a low bar to entry and by letting participants build apps based on their own interests.

This practice was established in the very first competition, Apps for Democracy, by organizer Peter Corbett of iStrategyLabs. He reasoned that "rules are the enemy of creativity and innovation. As soon as you say, 'Well, if you're a developer, you have to use this specific data set or you have to build this kind of app,' you all of a sudden winnow down the potential participants."[2]

While open-ended judging criteria are no guarantee of a high number of submissions, our survey of CACs shows that the competitions with the most entries did have open-ended judging criteria. This approach allows developers to build apps that solve problems in unorthodox ways, and provides judges maximum flexibility in selecting winners.

---

2. Peter Corbett as quoted in *http://sunlightfoundation.com/press/articles/2010/01/25/lessons-learned-two-apps-democracy-contests/*. He's referring to the guide to apps competitions he authored that can be found at *http://www.appsfordemocracy.org/guide-to-creating-your-own-apps-for-democracy/*

The drawback to this approach is that it encourages quantity instead of quality. When developers have no direction or standards to meet, there will be a certain number who build the simplest app possible and call it a day. In addition, developers who genuinely want to build something useful don't get any guidance.

The Targeted Approach

Organizers who use the targeted approach provide clear design principles. Their goal is to maximize the quality of the competition apps by directing participants to problems that need solving.

For example, the EPA's Apps for the Environment competition required all participants to address one of seven dictated principles for the EPA's future. These outcome-oriented principles, which included improving air quality and taking action on climate change, established practical guidelines for participants.

The winning apps were all designed by app development businesses and are still in use, an outcome that no other app competition we reviewed matched. The drawback to this approach is that it limits participation. The competition attracted just 38 submissions compared to the 80–100 submissions for more open-ended competitions. We've included a review of the pros and cons of open-ended vs. target rules in Table 6-1.

Table 6-1. Pros and cons of open-ended and targeted rules

	Pros	Cons	Best for
Open-ended	• Allows developers to build based on their own interests • May result in apps with a brand new approach to using data • Maximizes participation	• Apps tend to be of lower quality overall • May result in no apps that usefully solve problems • Provides no guidance to developers who want to build something genuinely useful	• Competitions where the goal is to maximize app entries
Targeted	• Results in higher quality apps • Provides guidance to developers	• Generates fewer submissions	• Competitions where the goal is to solve a specific problem or set of problems.

Judging Process

Winners can be chosen by public voting, judges or some combination of the two. The majority of apps competitions use a combination of the two because a judging panel brings technical expertise and star power, while a public voting component allows for community participation.

The three basic methods for organizing winner the selection process are:

- Judges winnow submissions down to finalists and allow public voting to determine placement. (Apps for Metro Chicago)
- Judges award all prizes except the popular choice award, which is selected by public voters. (Apps for Californians, NYC BigApps)
- Judges award all prizes. (Apps for America)

As always, choose a judging process that fits your goals. We've included a review of the pros and cons of different prize judging methods in Table 6-2.

Table 6-2. Pros and cons of prize judging methods

	Pros	Cons	Best for
Combined panel and public voting	• Engages a broader section of the public with the competition	• More expensive, because the website must be able to manage voting • Opens up the possibility of cheating • Winners tend to be decided by the developer with the best network instead of the best app	• Competitions focused on community and transparency issues • Well funded competitions • Competitions with the goal of maximizing awareness
Judges award all prizes but popular choice	• Allows public to engage with the competition without compromising the quality of the majority of winners	• More expensive, because the website must be able to manage voting • Opens up the possibility of cheating • Winners tend to be decided by the developer with the best network instead of the best app	• Competitions with the goal of maximizing awareness
Judges award all prizes	• Simplest	• No way for the public to engage with the competition	• Competitions with a small budget • Competitions that do not emphasize benefit to the community

Judge Selection

There are two approaches to selecting judges:

- Create a panel of local open government and tech entrepreneurs (Portland's Civic Apps)
- Create an anonymous panel chosen from within the organizing institution (Apps for the Environment; Apps for Californians)

There are benefits and drawbacks to both options. Creating a panel of local celebrities and tech stars can form a pillar of your communications strategy if the judges agree to use their professional and social media channels to promote the competition. Local judges are also helpful if an outcome is to energize the local tech start-up or developer community. Getting in front of a local tech entrepreneur or government official might be a good reason to join a CAC. The drawback is that recruiting local star judges requires a fair amount of time and energy and there is a high risk that busy judges drop out or don't vote at the last minute.

An internal panel is by far the easiest to recruit and manage. The drawback there is that you may get flack for a process isn't deemed transparent enough. Also, internal judges can't contribute as much in terms of recruiting participants as celebrity and tech star judges. We've included a review of the pros and cons of judging panel composition methods in Table 6-3.

Table 6-3. Pros and cons of judging panel composition methods

	Pros	Cons	Best for
Star Judges	• Drives press coverage • Drives social media buzz • Boost participation	• Time consuming to recruit and manage judges • Stars may drop out at the last minute	• Competitions with tech company partners who can provide judges • Well funded competitions • Competitions with the goal of maximizing awareness
Internal judges	• Simplest method • Ensures judge participation	• May lead to charges of lack of transparency • Doesn't create a communication benefit	• Competitions with a small budget • Competitions with the goal of solving a specific problem

Type of Eligible Apps: Mobile, Web, Tablet

Developers can build apps for a range of platforms, including mobile, web and tablet, but you may opt to limit eligible platforms.

There are several factors to consider. The most obvious is that any limits drive participation down. However, your goals might still make limits a good choice. For example, if your goal is to maximize the number of apps that benefit the community, restricting developers to web-based entries ensures maximum access by the public.

There is also a hidden time cost to accepting mobile entries: all apps built for Apple's iPhone must be accepted by the Apple Apps store before they can be downloaded and judged. Adding a third party to the judging process throws an element of uncertainty into the timeline. In addition, adding another hoop for developers to jump through has a negative impact on submissions.

The Apps for Californians competition devised an elegant solution to the challenge of judging mobile apps by partnering with ProgrammableWeb.com, an organization with an existing platform for hosting and testing apps. By simplifying judge access to apps for testing, ProgrammableWeb.com saved the Apps for Californians organizers a great deal of time, effort and reinvention of the wheel. We've included a review of the pros and cons of unrestricted and web-only platforms in Table 6-4.

Table 6-4. Pros and cons of unrestricted and web-only platforms

	Pros	Cons	Best for
Unrestricted platforms	• Maximizes participation • Mobile apps appeal to developers interested in selling the app after the close of the competition	• Difficult to download and judge apps for a range of devices • Apple iPhone apps must go through a lengthy third party process to appear in the Apple Apps store before they can be downloaded for judging • Tablet and smart phone apps limit usefulness to general public	• Competitions with the goal of maximizing participation • Competitions with a long enough time frame to allow iPhone apps to be considered
Web only	• Greatly simplifies the judging process • Maximizes usability for the general public	• Limits participation	• Competitions with small budgets • Competitions with the goal of maximizing benefit to the public

Participation Drivers: Events and Communications

The principles of market segmentation are a useful starting point here. First, identify the different groups you are trying to reach, then develop tactics to engage them.

For example, the main groups you want to engage might be software developers, students, municipal institutions, local non-profits, businesses and the general public. By approaching each group differently you can create the optimal mix of tactics. We've included a review of engagement tactics in Table 6-5.

Table 6-5. Communication tactics

Market Segment	Engagement Tactics	Broadcast Tactics
Software Developers	• Organize hackathons • Get on the agenda at tech and open government meet-ups • Present at public technology events like TechWeek	• Ask celebrity judges to promote the competition through their networks • Create a competition hash tag for Twitter • Create a facebook page
Students	• Contact professors at local universities and colleges and ask them to tell their students about the competition	• Post fliers on department bulletin boards • Put announcements in the student paper
Municipal Institutions	• Brainstorm ways to leverage internal resources with colleagues in other government departments	• Request department heads and the executive officials to promote the competition through their networks
Local non-profits and community advocates	• Reach out to foundations for introductions to local non-profits • Invite community groups to send representatives to brainstorm with developers at hackathons • Play "matchmaker" between developers and organizations interested in working on the same issues	• Tweet announcements to local foundations and non-profits • Post on facebook and non-profit facebook pages
Businesses	• Get on the agenda at local Chamber of Commerce Meetings • Reach out to established tech companies and start-ups for advice	• Get media coverage in the business press
Public voters	• Hold an ideas competition for people without developer skills • Have municipal sites direct visitors to vote for competition winners	• Get media coverage in local papers and weeklies • Encourage developers who submit apps to promote voting through their personal networks • Put out social media alerts on government social media channels during voting period

Next Chapter: Common Roadblocks

In the next chapter, we'll take a look at common roadblocks CAC organizers encounter so you can plan to avoid them.

CHAPTER 7

Common Roadblocks

All project directors are familiar with the feeling of slowly dawning horror when an unexpected issue crops up and threatens your timeline. In this section we highlight the issues that we stumbled over as we planned and ran the Apps for Metro Chicago competition (A4MC) in the hope that you can manage them better. These include:

- Competition app ownership
- Time needed to conduct the legal review of the rules
- Submission system and rules
- Screening out ineligible submissions
- Testing competition apps
- Preventing public voter cheating
- Dealing with the disgruntled

We also share how we handled the issues as they popped up, and tell a few good stories on ourselves.

Who Owns the App After the Competition Is Over?

This question appears in every competition's FAQ sheet, and with good reason. If the developer has to sign over rights to a competition submission, then their only chance of making money on their app is to win a prize.

Some competitions, including NYC BigApps, and Apps for Communities, tried to circle the square. They required free access to submitted apps on competition websites for one year. Developers maintained the right to sell the apps on other sites.

Others competitions, including Apps for Metro Chicago, required submissions to be free to the public for a year after the competition closed. Because the prize money for A4MC was funded in large part by charitable foundations, our primary goal had to be maximizing benefit to the public rather than support entrepreneurship. This situation made local tech companies much less enthusiastic about participating, since they would be giving their work away for free. Officially, a "further tweaked" version of the app could have been developed and sold aside from the one submitted to A4MC, but the line between the "A4MC" app and "further tweaked" wasn't made clear enough to overcome developer misgivings.

Your competition goals are the deciding factor behind the ownership decision. If your goal is to encourage entrepreneurship, then the builders should retain ownership. If your goal is to maximize public use of apps, then the builders should be required to make their apps free for a period of time. But as implied above, the source of the prize money may limit your ability to decide who owns the app.

Legal Review of the Rules

The legal implications of running a competition are extensive, so be sure to schedule enough time for a full legal review of the rules. Finalizing the rules for Apps for Metro Chicago required multiple rounds of review with partners. The whole process took four weeks—about three weeks longer than we anticipated.

We strongly recommended that all organizers retain an attorney to keep a mindful eye on the fine print. Legal issues you may encounter:

Local lottery issues
    Whenever prize money is involved, competition rules must comply with local lottery laws.

Liability
    Partners will want to ensure there is a clause indemnifying them from liability claims.

Ownership
    Potential entrants will want to know who owns the app during and after the competition.

Eligibility
    Whenever prize money is involved, competition rules must disqualify participants employed by the CAC organizers, partners and sponsors, as well as minors.

Submission System and Rules

If you choose to build your own competition website you'll need a system for accepting app submissions. The simplest and cheapest way to do this is to use an existing system like www.eventbrite.com, rather than building your own. We speak from experience on this one; we built the A4MC submission page from scratch and it was time consuming, buggy and expensive. Technical glitches that compromised access to the apps before and after judging and voting was one of our biggest hurdles.[1]

The submission requirements should be minimal: name, contact info, url, a brief description of the problem the app solves, the data set(s) used, and the names of any additional team members. If there is any additional eligibility criteria, like a partnership with an institution, it should be included also. You can also give participants the option to include more elaborate elements like a demo video.

Screening Out Ineligible Submissions

Apps can be ineligible for reasons ranging from copyright issues to functionality issues, and competition judges should not be relied on to master the intricacies of the eligibility rules. Build in an eligibility process run by the organizers to screen apps before handing off to the judges.

Apps for Metro Chicago developed a three step system for screening apps that moved the process along quickly.

First step: Did the developer follow the eligibility rules? Any apps that were not publicly available or could not be installed were eliminated here. We also eliminated apps with questionable authorship and connections to ineligible organizations. We also attempted to address copyright issues, regarding the name of the app and any images used.

Second step: Did they use at least one data set from the competition data portal, and use it correctly? On our app submission page we asked developers to identify the competition data set(s) they used. One of the reasons MCIC was asked to be the managing partner for the competition was so that we could curate the data—help developers understand it and make sure that it was used correctly (for example, were crime definitions used consistently?).

Third step: Can a person be reasonably expected to use the app? Apps with too many bugs or an incomprehensible user interface were disqualified in this step.

The apps that passed through the screening process were the only ones the judges tested.

Keep in mind that even an efficient screening process can take a great deal of time. We found it difficult to predict how much time was required and found ourselves pressed for time during the judging sessions. This issue was exacerbated by the fact that we gave ourselves only five days to manage the judging!

---

1. The initial competition manager at MCIC drew heavily upon Peter Corbett's "Guide to Creating Your Own Apps for Democracy" which can be found online at *http://www.appsfordemocracy.org/guide-to-creating-your-own-apps-for-democracy/*

We recommend building in at least a week—and preferably two or three—for the screening and judging process to compensate for the uncertainty. We thought we'd be able to partially mitigate the time crunch by screening apps as they came in, but since changes to the app could technically be carried out until the deadline, that didn't work for us. One way around this would be to "lock" the app—once submitted, no further changes are allowed.

Testing Competition Apps

Once you've identified the eligible apps the judges can begin their work. There are two ways to approach the judging process: bring the judges together to review the apps as a group, or allow each judge to conduct their review on their own time.

For Apps for Metro Chicago we wanted to make judging as easy as possible on our panels, so we decided to let them all review the apps on their own schedule. Unfortunately, this raised a number of sticky problems. Most of our judges didn't have all the devices necessary to test the apps. If they were confused by our judging criteria, they had to track someone down to explain it to them. And, of course, many of them simply lost track of time and weren't able to judge at all.

We strongly recommend convening the judges. Having everyone together in a room ensures that all the judges have access to the technology they need to test apps, it makes it easy to answer their questions, it improves participation and moves the process along quickly. Plus, it's much easier to plan.

In either case, make sure judges document their votes and reasoning. App developers will want this input to improve their app or to understand why their app didn't make the grade. You'll need it for proof that the contest wasn't rigged. Specific comments might be:"This app doesn't work on X platform", "I've seen this app before", "I tried it five times and couldn't get it to work." You'll need these comments, especially if the judges aren't at the awards ceremony or otherwise meeting with the developers.

Preventing Public Voter Cheating

If you build your CAC website in-house (as opposed to hiring the services of a vendor) and make public voting a part of the prize allocation process, you will need to take some precautions to minimize cheating. The competitors' high level of technical expertise and the prize amounts involved make cheating a real threat to the integrity of the competition.

Because we built our own platform for Apps for Metro Chicago, we had to spend a lot of time and effort designing systems to minimize cheating, yet we still got complaints.

If you decide to build a custom system, here are some methods to employ:

- Require voters to sign up for an account in order to vote. This way you can make sure that each email address only gets one vote and that temporary email addresses using the "+" character and an existing address can be disqualified.
- Incorporate a Captcha test to eliminate accounts created by an automated process.
- Require each voter to choose between 3-5 apps instead of just voting for one.
- Log as much information as you can about every vote. A spreadsheet with the IP addresses, timestamps and if possible the full headers (including the agent user string) sent with the voting HTTP request. In the event that you receive reports of cheating, you will have the documentation to show exactly what happened.
- We restricted our voting by IP address and eliminated votes we identified as fraudulent during the competition. This approach proved to be a mistake. For example, we eliminated dozens of votes that came from the employees of a single company. That decision alienated a lot of people who were initially very excited to participate.
- Tom Lee, Director of Sunlight Labs, recommends a different approach to weeding out voting cheats. In his view, "eliminating fraudulent votes is a forensic exercise performed after voting. This helps to ensure that fraud methods don't become more sophisticated as you locate and block them. With sufficient voting volume, even a simple histogram of vote times by entry will go a long way to identifying who's a human (who will tend to vote at particular times) and who's a robot."

Dealing with the Disgruntled

It's impossible to design and execute a flawless CAC that will leave everyone satisfied. Anything can go wrong. This list is not meant to be exhaustive, but will give you a taste of the diverse set of possible problems that could arise:

After judging, too few submissions qualify for public voting
Be sure your rules include what happens if not all prizes can be given away.

Developers disagree with judgment passed on their app
This is where it behooves you to keep copious records of screening criteria, judges' comments, and public votes. People get attached to their app and may take things personally. One contestant said "the fact that my app is not a finalist is bizarre." We received several questions about the judges' ranking system, and some participants took offense to judges' comments on an app. Be sure to let the judges know if the notes they are taking will be shared. But also be prepared for developers who disagree with the judges' comments.

Developers disagree with judgment passed on someone else's app

Developers often test other submissions that won or scored higher than their own, and tend to find the other app wanting. Be sure your rules specify whether screening, judging and public voting records can be shared with people other than the author/developer.

There are third-party complaints about the legality of an app

The name of an app may contain trademark or copyrighted references—"TransitFacebook" or "FindStarbucks" are representative of the kinds of titles we encountered. In another case, we were threatened with a lawsuit on the grounds that a prize-winning app was illegally "acting" as a realtor under Illinois law.

Next Chapter: The Long Game

With any luck, this guide will help you build an effective and successful CAC. But an awesome Civic Apps Competition is just one way government can support the development and growth of a community of practice around open government data.

In our next chapter, we'll cover other ways you can engage your community with open government data.

CHAPTER 8

Building on Success

A civic apps competition is a terrific way to get people excited about open government data, but a single event—no matter how amazing—isn't enough to sustain lasting interest.

In this chapter, we're going to cover different tactics to keep the energy going. Although Apps for Metro Chicago ended last year, we are still active in Chicago's OGD community and have our eye on efforts to keep A4MC's energy going. We share the best ones here.

We've divided them into three groups: engaging in conversations, participating in events and continuing to build apps. To keep it interesting, we're including ideas from people who are currently running successful and interesting events.

Engaging in Conversation

Participants poured a lot of energy into your competition and they want to know that you appreciate them. The best way to do that is to continue to engage them in conversations about open government data in your community. Face-to-face conversations are a good start, but there are three good options for scaling those conversations up: blogging, Twitter and email lists.

Blogging

The key benefit of blogging is that it's informal. You can write in your own voice and focus on the ideas that you think are the most interesting. The best blogs make readers feel like they're hearing the author expound on ideas over a couple of drinks at the local pub. Some of our favorite blogs are:

- www.ascentstage.com, by Chicago Chief Technology Officer John Tolva.
- *http://open.nasa.gov/about/* is a bit more formal, but space apps are just plain interesting.
- Sunlight Labs, a part of the Sunlight Foundation (a non-profit organization focused on the digitization and accessibility of government data) is a great source of blogs about all things OGD (*http://sunlightlabs.com/blog/*)
- Logan Kleier, the Chief Information Officer at the City of Portland, has an insightful blog at Code for America: (*http://codeforamerica.org/author/logan-kleier/*)

Twitter

Not everyone has the time or energy to blog, but pretty much anyone can get the hang of Twitter in about 60 seconds.

Twitter is a great way to let other people find all the interesting ideas, events and articles for you. The key is to start by following interesting people, rather than trying to be interesting yourself. Whenever you read something interesting, retweet it and voila! You are part of the conversation.

Twitter is a great platform for making yourself available to answer questions. Developers tend to be heavy Twitter users, so connecting with them on their preferred platform makes them happy and makes your competition's email inbox a little easier to manage. Follow hashtags such as #gov20, #opendata, #fedstats, #opengov and #govdata.

We follow lots of folks, but here are some of our favorites:

- @digiphile: Alexander Howard's Twitter feed. He covers open government data for O'Reilly Media and speaks to data, privacy, policy, and most aspects of open data.
- @govfresh: Up-to-the-minute information on open government news and events.
- @opengov: The official Twitter account of the White House Open Government Initiative will keep you up to speed on the policy and politics of open government.

- @JeanneHolm: Jeanne is an Evangelist for Data.gov and a Knowledge Architect at NASA.
- @SarahSchacht: She's funny and she's all over open gov, particularly in the American West.

Email Lists

You collected the emails of your participants, right? You should take care of these people, and giving them access to government meetings and events is a great way to do it. Invite them to interesting official events and send them breaking news updates on policy. Just be sure you don't get spammy—there's no quicker way to lose someone's interest.

Participating in Events

Hold Constituent Meetings

Holding public hearing sessions is a powerful—and relatively cheap—tool government officials have at their disposal. Even though you won't be able to take action on every idea, listening to what people say about your open data efforts demonstrates your commitment to the community. And, of course, it's a great channel for learning what's really on people's minds.

Attend Events Hosted by Other Open Data and Open Government Groups

During the course of running your CAC, you probably identified the local groups interested in open data. Put their meetings on your calendar and make an appearance every so often. It shows you're willing, and it's a lot less stress than hosting or presenting.

Conferences

Attending and presenting at conferences is a time honored way to become part of a larger conversation. Local conferences are cheapest and easiest to attend and participate in, but there is one national conference on each coast worth your attention:

The O'Reilly Strata Conference: A business and government crowd talking about "the changes brought to technology and business by big data, data science, and pervasive computing."

OpenGov West: Community stakeholders, government and business "come together to discuss transparency, collaboration and participation."

A good way to find local conferences is through local Meetup groups (*www.meet-up.com*). Most major cities have an "open government" Meetup group. What's great about Meetups is that they're organized so that people who would otherwise not run into each other get to meet.

An opengov Meetup is likely to include folks from government, foundations, for-profit software and technology businesses, community organizations, graphic design companies. Although new strategies and applications for OGD are commonly the topic of interest, information about local conferences where apps are showcased or software discussed can be had.

Continuing to Build Apps

Partner with Other Open Government Events and Projects

There's no need for you to plan every open government data event in your city; try inviting other organizations to host. Code for America and Random Hacks of Kindness (all profiled below) host hackathons across the country. Universities, colleges, and open government groups run hackathons. Promote or assisting another event is a win-win.

Hackathons and Events

A hackathon is a gathering of developers to collaboratively build software. They typically last between 24 and 48 hours, although shorter meetings are also possible. Running a good hackathon is a project in and of itself, and you can find a good guide here: *http://bendoernberg.posterous.com/67675074.*

Traditionally, hackathons have been very developer-centric; participants are there to have fun and build something interesting—not to solve a specific problem or create a tool intended for wide use. Over the past year or two, organizers have made efforts to shape that are more solution oriented. DataKind, Code for America and Random Hacks of Kindness have pioneered effective methods for organizing events that help developers identify useful problems to solve and make those solutions sustainable.

Rather than try to capture their magic, we asked an organizer from each organization to share their methods in their own words.

Interview with Jake Porway, Executive Director of DataKind

DataKind is a nonprofit that connects data scientists with non-profits to better collect, analyze and visualize data. We bring together teams of pro-bono data scientists who want to do more with their spare time, and we pair them up with non-profits who have data, but don't have the skills or awareness to build on it.

We have two ways of doing this:

DataDives

These are souped-up hackathons—weekend events that connect three non-profit organizations with local data scientists to solve a specific data problem. We invite local non-profit groups to apply to be one of the three, and we select the final groups based on the quality of their question and their data. We also rank groups on their organization's commitment to using data as a core part of their operations so we know we're going to have an impact.

One of our biggest challenges is helping our three non-profit organizations frame a workable problem. So before the event starts we assign each organization a data ambassador. Our data ambassadors are local volunteers, and they serve as liaisons between the non-profits and the volunteer developers. Their job is to work with the organizations to review their data, frame some big questions and narrow them down into actionable tasks.

What's nice is that this is a learning process for both groups. What inevitably happens is that the organization talks about what they want, and then the data ambassador finds their data can't answer the original question, but can do some other useful things. Then the organization usually says, "Wow, we didn't even think of that, but now that you mention it, we can add in some new data to help!" So it's an iterative process where the organization learns what the data can do, and the ambassador learns more about what the organization really needs.

During the event, the ambassador keeps the developers working on the right questions. Of course, the question you go in with isn't always the question you end up with. Issues always pop up, anomalies erupt, and the process evolves. It's important to have a representative of the non-profit at the event to answer questions.

At the end of the event there are presentations on what everyone did to wrap things up and show off. However, what we've found is that the vast majority of these groups don't just say "great, task done, job over"—instead they're so inspired by the collaborations that they want to continue working in more depth with the volunteers. We've seen that even without our prompting, the groups want to stay connected. We help facilitate that through our second form of engagement, the DataCorps.

DataCorps projects

DataCorps projects are like long-term pro-bono projects that can be done remotely over a number of months. They can be one person or a team. DataDives aren't designed to solve a big problem—there's no big problem you're going to solve in 24 hours with strangers. What they do is get people excited, build connections, and act as a filter for very engaged volunteers and nonprofits that are interested in the data. DataCorps helps connect those teams and makes it possible for their work to go forward. Right now we just do it through your standard array of open source tools, like Dropbox and email.

One DataCorps team worked with DC Action for Children, an organization that tracks key indicators of children's health and wellbeing. Every year their Kids Count initiative publishes a huge amount of data about child wellbeing, but it's usually in the form of a large PDF. They wanted to do more with the data than just publish it, so the DC DataDive team, headed up by Sisi Wei, a graphic designer with the Washington Post, built an interactive map. Users can scroll over neighborhoods and see all kinds of demographic information.

The team loved the work so much they wanted to keep building it out to make it a real piece of software. A team of six has continued to work on it, they meet once a month for afternoon DataDives, and fill in work in between as needed.

It's pretty incredible: these volunteers chose to do a 6 month engagement in their spare time. They do it because they know they are building something genuinely useful for the DC Action for Kid. If this project works out, building this kind of interactive visualization will be the model for all Kids Counts throughout the nation.

Interview with Veronica Ludwig, Code for America's IdeaHack organizer

When I met with the Code For America fellows, they told me about Code Across America—events around the country that bring citizens together on the same day. CFA wanted a lot of community members involved—not just developers. So I told them a hackathon wasn't ideal because that's a developer event. Most folks who aren't developers wouldn't know what a hackathon is and once they found out they'd feel it was a waste of their time since they can't code. So that's where IdeaHack came from—we wanted to get all these different folks together in a room, feeling comfortable and sharing ideas. That was our main goal: reaching out to community members who are passionate about the city and making it better. The best way to get people involved is to reach the people who are already doing things on their own and then tapping their networks.

Christopher Whitaker and Josh Kalov were the main volunteers for IdeaHack. Along with the CFA Fellows, we pulled together our networks and created a targeted invite list with attention to the percentage of types of people. We wanted a majority of community leaders and city officials with designers and developers in smaller numbers. We also decided to make the event invite-only because we wanted to bring together a diverse group of people who all shared a civic mentality.

It worked out so much better than we thought it was going to—we sold out in 12 hours and then people started inviting people. We wound up going a little over capacity with 97 people instead of the 80 we were shooting for—a great success for a new event!

We gathered a committee of people to help organize the "day of" event and met with them a week before the event to ideahack the ideahack. We used that time to identify our facilitators, organizers and event managers and set the topics and the structure of the day. We wound up running the event in the form of an unconference, which allowed attendees to engage with eachother throughout the entire event.

After the event was over we gave the original organizers a few weeks to recover and then met to talk about keeping the momentum up. We were getting lots of emails from people who had loved the event and others who had missed it and wanted to know if there would be another one. In this post ideahack, we decided to make future events significantly smaller because smaller crowds are best for exchanging ideas. We also wanted to create a stable, structured resource for people because even well motivated people need structure to channel their work.

Originally we were going to do ideahacks every month and have a regular hack night once a week. But we couldn't get someone to commit to facilitating those events. So instead we talked with the local Open Gov group and and they started a weekly hack night. So instead of competing against each other, we decided to work with the other groups to accomplish the same goals. This was really helpful, because no one had to take on additional work and no one was scared away by the initial start-up effort. These events are still going on and new people keep on joining the work we started.

Interview with Willow Brugh, Director and James Carlson, Advisor, Random Hacks of Kindness/ Geeks without Bounds

Geeks Without Bounds (GWOB) was launched on October 10th, 2010, as "an international coalition of problem solvers working together to assist people whose survival is improved through access to technology or communications in instances of violence, neglect, or catastrophe." After hosting a number of hackathons in partnership with Random Hacks of Kindness throughout 2011 and seeing encouraging results, our team noticed that most of the projects we started were just a flash in the pan. What could we do to keep teams together? What could we do to help them turn into sustainable communities—and give some of the value back to their open source roots?

We brought this challenge to RHOK who agreed; we became a RHOK sustainability partner and began to envision a sustaining accelerator for the projects that come out of hackathons. We call it the Accelerator for Humanitarian Projects.

RHOK has a fabulous history of globally organizing hackathons for humanity; the Geeks without Bounds accelerator takes ideas (primarily, but not always) from hackathons and helps turn them into sustainable businesses, programs or products. While many of these projects can come from a RHOK event, they can also come from other hackathons and do-athons. The key is that the teams are committed and willing to dive deep to bring their project to fruition. The GWOB team works with the hackathon organizers to find projects that seem most suited for future sustainability, and which have a humanitarian mission. We apply a rigorous evaluation to these projects, so that we can find projects that are most likely to succeed.

We then invite the teams responsible for those projects to join our accelerator program. These teams get six months of mentorship in idea generation, presentation, technical problem-solving, legalese, and funding. At the end of the process, they have a good business model; some teams choose to form a nonprofit, a corporation, or have their technology or idea get acquired by another organization for its mission.

We need to begin taking the incredible energy released by hackathons and applying it to build a new world. After a three-month selection process, the first teams have been announced—FourTeachers, which brings a platform for lesson plan sharing for instructors, BioMedLink which helps the developing world find affordable medical devices appropriate for their climate and culture, and WaterMe which provides and API for drought.

Each of these teams is currently consulting with a variety of mentors, who are advising them on the development of their business model and solution. We hope to have results for the evaluation of the wider community later this year and early next year. Results and progress are being tracked via the gwob.org site, and we often open up our G+ hangouts.

Closing Thoughts

This book is full of details, ideas and recommendations, but as you pick and choose the elements of your own CAC, we want you to keep your big picture goals in mind. In the short term you need to generate buzz, excitement and participation; in the long term you want government data to continue being used.

Government data contains a wealth of information whose usefulness goes beyond what can be done in a CAC. Since CACs have created few apps that have a reasonable shelf-life, the emphasis should be on building the right kind of competition in order to address the goals of accountability, government efficiency and innovation (we might even suggest that these are three different kinds of competitions). We do NOT recommend a splashy competition that can run into the hundreds of thousands of dollars. As we demonstrated, that's an extremely expensive way to announce "government data is now open for business." A shorter competition with sustainable elements built in is preferable.

Accountability

The generation of civic coders coming of age over the last several years has a new wealth of open source tools, social media outlets to tell stories ("like," "follow," "donate") and online ability to "join" political movements. Their technical skills and ease in navigating new promotional tools makes them an invaluable partner in addressing social and political problems. These skills coupled with generative issue organizations on the ground could be a powerful force unleashed through CAC's. We suggest that sustainable elements such as hack salons, support for sustained match-making, and pairing between civic coders and those with problems and political voices needs to be in place to address issues of accountability and democratic access.

While a plethora of self-organizing tools for civic coders exist (everything from international open data conferences, to local Meetups, to shared files on GitHub), the network of data-driven organizations who have been delivering data solutions to nonprofits for decades is less visible. The National Neighborhood Indicators Partnership (NNIP) is one; the Open Indicators Consortium is another. We urge local CACs to reach out to find these local groups and bring them into the competition (MCIC is a member of NNIP). The experience of these groups with government data and with civic groups on the ground should be harnessed to deliver the community of practice. This community then, together, can achieve a voice for accountability.

The case study for iFindit demonstrates that CACs can create a space for non-developers to understand the potential for open data to address problems they encounter and get practical experience in how an app (or web platform) is developed. Developers can use experience with civic groups to inform the way they develop insights with government data. This cross-pollination drives use over time.

Government Efficiency

We also suggest that apps competitions have made more visible the tension between "government as platform" ("just give us the data") and the need for apps that can create real value for government and citizens. Procurement rules are a tough nut when it comes to having government be able to adopt public-created apps, so there does need to be some way for government to create value for itself. Since software developers aren't always likely to know the problem set faced by government staffers, just releasing the data (government-as-platform) doesn't necessarily solve problems of government efficiency. Without government apps the long-run viability of the gov-as-platform possibilities is attenuated. When the champion Chief Data Officer or Chief Technology Officer goes away, who is the champion? We suggest that if apps have been created that help government departments do their work better, it's more likely that internal support for open data will continue.

Ways to ensure this include: addressing procurement regulations head of time, setting up the competition rules so that government staffers can enter the competition (even if not "win"), creating specific hack salons where government staffers meet with civic coders. An idea we had, but did not follow through on, was to create a "winning category" specifically for addressing government-identified problems (e.g., the truck route finder discussed above).

For-Profit Innovation

Software developers get hired based on projects and connections. CAC's can provide a path for student developers and professionals transitioning into the tech field to build out their portfolio and make connections with local developers and firms. That's why we recommend local judges from the for-profit tech community. Connections and partnerships formed in a CAC can strengthen local technology businesses.

The harder problem is that local civic data in and of itself doesn't necessarily provide enough juice upon which to build a for-profit business app. Realistically the application would have to scale to other geographies in order to be profitable. SpotHero, which won A4MC, is an example. A platform to connect those who need and those who have parking spaces, SpotHero is a technology that almost certainly needs to scale by using other jurisdictions' data (and that data is increasingly available) to become profitable. *National* government data such as 401(k) and 403(b) performance, (used by BrightScope to rate retirement plans), gives much more raw material upon which to build private sector business than can any set of local civic data.

The advent of cross-jurisdictional platforms and initiatives such as Code for America's multi-city Open311 platform (and 311 Labs),[1] and cities.data.gov (an initiative among several municipal Chief Information Officers)[2] promises to perhaps develop a richer set of data upon which to build private-sector activity with local data. We're dubbing this "Big Data from the Ground Up."

We're excited for a democratic future where more data powers more knowledge. We see the ingredients for this coming from a partnership among civic coders, community leaders, and government staffers. Civic Apps Competitions are a means by which to introduce ourselves.

---

1. *http://codeforamerica.org/category/open311/*

2. *http://www.data.gov/communities/cities*

About the Authors

Kate Eyler-Werve specializes in helping organizations adapt to disruptive technologies and ideas. When Walmart decided to go green, Kate designed and led campaigns to engage their 1.2 million employees with sustainability. When Mayor Rahm Emanuel decided to make Chicago more transparent, Kate led the launch team for the 2011 Apps for Metro Chicago Competition. She is looking for the next disruptive idea to play with.

Virginia Carlson, Ph.D. is a national figure in the role of information resources and their role in harnessing information for urban revitalization. She has developed and applied her expertise in a variety of settings, including: identifying data sources for the State of Illinois Index of Leading Indicators; constructing economic indicators for redevelopment options in Gorj County, Romania; identifying key data intervention points for federal data as the Deputy Director for Data Policy at the Brookings Institution's Urban Markets Initiative; and designing the strategic information approach for the campaign to induce The Boeing Company to move its headquarters to Chicago. She is a member of the Board of Directors for the Association of Public Data Users.

Have it your way.

O'Reilly eBooks

- Lifetime access to the book when you buy through oreilly.com
- Provided in up to four DRM-free file formats, for use on the devices of your choice:
  PDF, .epub, Kindle-compatible .mobi, and Android .apk
- Fully searchable, with copy-and-paste and print functionality
- Alerts when files are updated with corrections and additions

oreilly.com/ebooks/

Safari Books Online

- Access the contents and quickly search over 7000 books
  on technology, business, and certification guides
- Learn from expert video tutorials, and
  explore thousands of hours of video
  on technology and design topics
- Download whole books or chapters
  in PDF format, at no extra cost,
  to print or read on the go
- Get early access to books as they're being written
- Interact directly with authors of upcoming books
- Save up to 35% on O'Reilly print books

See the complete Safari Library at safari.oreilly.com

O'REILLY®